Beyond the Bleachers

The Art of Parenting Today's Athletes

David Canning Epperson, Ph.D.

and George A. Selleck, Ph.D.

Authors of
From the Bleachers with Love:
Advice to Parents with Kids in Sports

Library of Congress Cataloging-in-Publication Data:
Epperson, David C., 1932—
Selleck, George A., 1934—
       Beyond the Bleachers.—1st ed.
          p.   cm.
       ISBN   0-9672854-1-0
       1. Parenting. 2. Self-Improvement. I. Title.
       2000

This book is available in quantity at special discounts for your group or
organization. For information, contact:

   Alliance Publications
   P.O. Box 1429
   Sugar Land, TX 77478

   Phone (281) 565-2234
   Fax (281) 565-2224

Designed by Jody Boles.
Copyedited by Janice Hunt.

ACKNOWLEDGMENTS

The hundreds of parents, coaches, athletes, and sports administrators with whom we have consulted about this project over the past several years have inspired us to provide the tools for sports parents to more thoughtfully guide their children through the world of sports. In this book we have chosen to share with our readers case studies based upon real-life sports parenting episodes that these "informants" have related. We thank them for helping point the way - *beyond the bleachers* – and into the heart of the family, where sports can serve as a common ground upon which parents and children meet to share enriching athletic moments.

We also want to recognize the contributions our own children have made to our understanding of sports parenting. Like so many children, ours were too frequently subjected to less-than-ideal sports parenting. Their impatience with our well meaning but all too often awkward "support" helped raise our consciousness about many of the issues in this book. One of us recalls with great clarity his daughter running past the bleachers and shouting for everyone to hear, "Shut up, Dad!" in response to her father's well-intended "instructional commentary." That episode, along with many others, can be understood as initial sources of inspiration for this sports parenting project. We both learned just how important it is to let your children's life in sports be their own. We discovered how critical it is to "be there," but on your children's terms, not your own. Therefore, we would like to acknowledge our children's contributions to our understanding and invite them to accept this book as a belated atonement for our sports parenting "sins."

Also we would like to express our deep gratitude to our editor, Jim Kestner, who has brought to this project a level of sophistication about how to communicate with sports parents that has added immeasurably to the quality of our product.

This book is dedicated to our children,
Anna Kelley, Lara Sweeney, John, Alison, and Peter Selleck
who have inspired us to challenge sports parents
to go beyond the bleachers where
enriching athletic moments can be found

CONTENTS

INTRODUCTION

HOW TO BECOME AN
EFFECTIVE SPORTS PARENT

What was sports like when you were a kid? For those of us who grew up in the 1930s and 1940s sports meant getting together with our friends in a vacant lot or a park and playing until it was too dark to see the ball.   We didn't have fancy equipment or uniforms, and for the most part, the only involvement our parents had was to make sure we came home for dinner when called. When we were growing up in the '30s and '40s, out of necessity we created our own sports activities without the assistance of either coaches or parents. Marty Miller captures the fun-filled nature of youth sports in our time when he writes:

> I tell my grandchildren about my sandlot days of baseball. When I was their age my school chums got together every day after school and played baseball in any open space we could find in the neighbor-hood – school yards, streets, alleys, backyards and vacant lots. We didn't have much equipment. The kid with the ball and bat was in. We chose up sides. We set the rules. First base was the tree, the bush was second and the sewer cover was third. We used "take it over" often and a batted ball through the Murphy's window was an out and an out-of-there as fast as our little legs could take us. We didn't practice; we wouldn't have tolerated throwing drills, hitting drills, infield drills, outfield drills. We played the game and got better at it the longer we played. What fun and excitement! (*Applying Sociology: Making a Better World,* Allyn & Bacon, forthcoming 2000)

As we enter the new millennium "it's a new ball game" for sports parents. Youth sports have become *adult driven* rather than *child driven*. As a result, the rules of the parenting game have changed. This book is an effort to help you understand how to play this new game with joy, intelligence, and effectiveness, so that your family sports experiences preserve the best features of the "good old days" while capitalizing on all the opportunities that modern sports have to offer.

TAKING ADVANTAGE OF TODAY'S BOUNTIFUL SPORTS OPPORTUNITIES

Children and families today have an unprecedented range of athletic options. The richness of youth sports opportunities available today to both boys and girls is remarkable. They have more opportunities to participate in sports, have greater access to good and safe facilities and equipment, and are trained by better prepared coaches than ever before.

The benefits of these new developments come with significant costs, however. In the world of adult driven youth sports, children are often denied the opportunity to take charge of their own sports experiences. When we were kids, we learned to solve our own problems. We learned to be creative in constructing our games. And we learned to forgive ourselves and our teammates when we made errors. Scoreboards, trophies, championships, all-star teams, scholarships, high priced shoes, and uniforms were irrelevant. There was a purity about sports in those days that seems to have gotten lost in the shadow of college scholarships, enormous professional salaries, and outrageous behavior by high profile athletes, coaches, and owners.

While it is neither possible nor desirable to return to "the good old days," there are some advantages to remembering what sports are all about, what they can become in the lives of children and their families. When parents make the effort to equip themselves to lead their children through the world of sports in a positive and constructive way, the playing field raises spirits, teaches lessons, strengthens families, and enlivens communities.

CREATING EMPOWERING SPORTS EXPERIENCES

Today's successful sports parent isn't necessarily the mom or dad who guides a child to the winner's circle or to the ranks of high paid professional athletes. Rather, it is the parent who has *learned to use the available youth sports resources to provide empowering experiences for his or her children.* We use the term empowering to refer to those experiences that help make kids feel equipped to shape or control their own sports experiences. For kids, this sense of control comes through learning how to set goals, make decisions, and solve problems. It comes through feeling deeply involved in what they are doing and closely connected to those with whom they are doing it.

Because the heavy adult presence and highly structured activities of today's youth sports programs have a tendency to reduce the natural learning opportunities that child-driven sports present, it is important for you, your children, their coaches, and other sports team parents to join together to create these growth-enhancing opportunities.

OFFERING AN ANTIDOTE TO A TOXIC CULTURE

For kids, part of growing up means trying to establish their own identity. Frequently, this means rebelling against the control that parents and other adults try to exert over them. Sometimes it means acting out against authority or engaging in activities that are neither wholesome nor growth-enhancing.

The world of advertising and entertainment are all too ready to embrace our children by appealing to their needs to escape accountability and protest against adult "interference." The adolescent pop culture reflects this escape from authority, with its affinity for tobacco, alcohol, drugs, reckless sex, outrageous dress, tattoos, body piercing, loud and suggestive music, and other "in-your-face" challenges to adults whom they perceive to be standing in the way of their freedom.

A family-centered sports culture that includes respectful, caring, and well equipped parents can do much to counter these toxic influences. Sports can become a sanctuary where parents and coaches provide young people with opportunities to take charge of their lives in positive ways. Sports can become an antidote to those forces that cause so many young people to feel like they have little control over their lives.

CREATING A FAMILY-CENTERED SPORTS CULTURE

In *From the Bleachers with Love: Advice to Parents with Kids in Sports* we identify 52 principles that can help parents ensure that their children's sports experiences are uplifting and empowering.

Throughout our nearly 60 years of experience in sports we have learned from our conversations with children in each generation that for sports to be fun and exciting it is essential that kids feel they are in control of their experiences. *This book, which is a companion to* From the Bleachers with Love, *is dedicated to helping parents create a climate that offers all sports participants – athletes, coaches, officials, parents, and spectators – the opportunity to have joyful, inspiring, growth-enhancing sports experiences.*

HOW TO USE THIS BOOK

This book provides case studies, skill development exercises, discussion questions, and self assessment exercises to help you develop the parenting tools that will allow you to participate in creating positive sports experiences for your children and your family. By developing these skills you will be better equipped to restore the best of the "good old days." At the same time you will be able to take full advantage of the rich range of opportunities that today's sports environment provides you to teach your children life lessons.

Each chapter of the book begins with a case study based in the fictional Hawkinses. These realistic case studies illustrate various challenges that you may very well face as you guide your children through the world of sports. Please do not view these challenges as *problems*; instead, see them as *opportunities* to learn valuable skills that will make your sports parenting more effective and your family life more rewarding. In each chapter we

- Identify the skills you will need to address each sports parenting challenge;

- Offer advice about how to develop and apply those skills;

- Outline an exercise that will help you sharpen the skills; and

- List a series of questions that encourage you to examine your own readiness to address the issues related to each challenge.

We believe that this format provides an effective and interesting way for you to improve your own skills and engage the entire family in shaping your sports experiences.

MASTERING THE KEYS TO POSITIVE SPORTS PARENTING

The chapters in this book are organized around six keys to positive sports parenting:

- Charting Your Family's Sports Future
- Achieving Self Awareness Through Sports
- Helping Your Children Use Sports to Learn Life's Lessons
- Creating a Supportive Sports Climate
- Developing a Compassionate Sports Family
- Assuming Leadership in Your Children's Sports Community

Whereas *From the Bleachers with Love: Advice to Parents with Kids in Sports* focuses upon the *principles* of positive sports parenting. This companion volume focuses upon *how to* become a positive sports parent.

This book is not intended to be read from beginning to end, although you may certainly do that if you choose. Rather, it is designed to be used as a resource as you address or anticipate various challenges in your role as a sports parent.

As you move through the chapters, we encourage you to take time to reflect upon the questions being raised. Because we have tried to supply you with a framework for finding ways of coping with challenges, rather than cut-and-dried answers, your solutions must be shaped to fit your family's circumstances and reflect your unique family values.

The path to positive sports parting is not one you walk alone. Rather, it is a joint venture between you and everyone who is a member of your children's youth sports community. Remember, you cannot create a positive sports climate by yourself. *It takes a village to raise an athlete.* With this book, you can take first steps toward equipping yourself, your family, and your sports community with the skills to create a "village" where children are empowered by the leadership of enlightened, caring, and effective sports parents.

Meet the Hawkins Family

Patrick and Alecia Hawkins are dedicated parents who place a high priority on family. Patrick and Alecia's work schedules allow them to share in many of their children's sports activities.

Although Patrick was active in high school sports — especially football, where he was part of a team that won a state championship — he was not talented enough to win a college scholarship.

When his children were little, Patrick enjoyed playing on his company's softball team, but now he doesn't feel that their activities allow him the time to do this. Patrick doesn't really mind, though. Every time he watches his children compete, he gets just as excited as if it were him out there.

Alecia had few opportunities to participate in sports, partly because her father — a farmer — felt that sports were a waste of time. If she were pressed, she would probably say that she wouldn't mind if her kids were a little less "sports-crazy." However, she also feels like she missed out on something as a child because of not participating in organized sports. She wants her children to be able to have a wider range of experiences than she did, so she's willing to put up with the late dinners and endless chauffeuring duties that come with being a sports mom.

Patrick and Alecia have a son, Darren, and a daughter, Rochelle. Both children have been active in school and club sports for many years. Darren is a high school junior. He is an outstanding player who has a serious chance of becoming a scholarship athlete.

Rochelle is a high school sophomore. A bit of a tomboy as a child, Rochelle enjoys playing many sports. Rochelle's interests don't stop at sports, however. She's basically one of those kids who wants to do everything and be everywhere.

The following situations present problems designed to help you think about (1) the role you want sports to play in your family's life, and (2) the skills you need in order to resolve these and similar challenges that might arise during the course of your family's sports experiences. As you carefully study each case and complete the accompanying exercises, your family will develop a set of skills that will better enable you to communicate about your problems and effectively resolve them.

HOW TO DETERMINE YOUR
FAMILY SPORTS VALUES

Darren slumps into his chair with a sigh. "I can't believe it, Dad! Coach told us at practice today that Robert quit."

"There goes the season," Patrick replies, unthinkingly.

Alecia gives her husband a warning look. "That must be pretty disappointing for you, Darren," she says, trying to comfort her son. "Robert has been your training partner for years."

"What got into him?" Patrick blurts out. "How can he blow a chance at a $100,000 scholarship? What a dumb move!"

"He told Charles that he's burned out on sports and just wants to hang out with his friends — the guys who think it's cool to cruise around looking for action," Darren complains, as he storms out of the room muttering something about "traitors."

"He's pretty steamed," Patrick says.

"I'll say," Alecia replies. "And you didn't exactly help things out with your comments!"

What are the values that Darren is revealing in his reactions to Robert's decision? What does Robert seem to value? What values do Patrick and Alecia display in their responses? And finally, what are the values that are reflected in Alecia's responses to Darren and Patrick? How important is it for families to share common sports values?

IDENTIFYING VALUES

Each of us has a set of values that strongly influences our behavior. It is common for family members to share many sports values but differ on others. Since these values influence how each of you approaches sports, it is important to have a clear understanding of your children's and your partner's values as well as an understanding of your own orientation to sports. These values are the foundation upon which you build your family sports culture.

The Key to Identifying Your Values

To identify the values that govern your sports experiences, you need to ask yourself two questions: "What aspects of sports are most important to me?" and "Why are they important?" The following exercise will help you and your family answer these questions.

EXERCISE

Invite each family member to jot down answers to the following:

• What three sports figures do you most admire for the values they reflect on and off the playing field? (These can be high-profile sports figures, local athletes or coaches, or even friends or family members.) List at least three things that you admire about each of these individuals.

• What specific aspect of sports do you most enjoy? For example, is it the competition, watching your children or friends play, getting together with others, or something else? Why do you think you enjoy this particular part of sports so much?

• Comparing the time you spend on sports to other parts of your life, would you say that you spend more, less, or about the same amount of time on sports as most people? If it's considerably more than the average person, why do you spend that much time on sports? (In other words, do you feel the time is well spent because it's something the entire family enjoys, because it may result in athletic scholarships, because it encourages physical fitness, etc.?)

• What part of your sports participation reflects what you enjoy most, not just what you think you should want or what others may expect of you?

Discussion:

Begin by having each family member look for the patterns that emerge in their answers. (For example, maybe you thought winning was something that was very important to you, but the characteristics you find most attractive in the sports models you listed suggest that winning is not as important as being loyal, upbeat, or a good team player.)

After everyone has had time to think about their answers, compare answers (noting similarities and differences) as you discuss which values are most important in your family.

SELF-ASSESSMENT

• Based upon the common values that have been revealed in your family discussions, what features of a youth sports program would you say seem most important to your family? Make a list and ask your family if they feel the list is accurate.

• If you were to give one of your children's coaches a description of the values your family would like to see emphasized in their program, what would you highlight? How would you express your position in a way that would not be viewed as a challenge to either the coach's values or authority?

2

HOW TO INCLUDE SPORTS ISSUES IN FAMILY MEETINGS

"Guess what, Mom?" Darren exclaims. "Coach Jones talked to me today about trying out for his team! He said he's watched me play, and with my speed and strength, I should be able to become a starter by the time the season begins. Isn't that great?"

Alecia looks concerned. "But Darren, you're already so busy. Can you fit this in?"

"Yeah, no problem," Darren responds. "Wait till Dad hears about this! He'll be jazzed!"

However, Patrick greets Darren's news with a lack of enthusiasm. "Gee, Darren," Patrick says, "I'm not sure if we can come up with the money or the time to support you in another sport. Besides, wouldn't a lot of your games conflict with Rochelle's? I'll tell you what — let's have a family meeting tomorrow night and discuss it."

What can Alecia and Patrick do to make sure no one's needs are neglected because of their children's sports involvement?

CONDUCTING FAMILY MEETINGS

Regular family meetings give you an opportunity to address the needs of your family and to work together to find ways to meet these needs. However, it takes some practice to make sure family meetings stay positive and focus on meeting family needs rather than airing complaints. To conduct an effective meeting, you need to:

- Set and enforce meeting times;
- Work with family members to select agenda items;
- Give everyone a chance to be heard;
- Apply conflict-resolution skills (See p. xx for a discussion of these skills);
- Keep meetings on track.

Keeping a Meeting on Track:

1. Post your meeting agenda in advance (on the bulletin board or refrigerator).
2. Give assignments ahead of time ("Carl, we'd like you to be able to tell us what you have planned this week and what areas you will need us to help you with.").
3. Start the meeting on time and stick to an agreed-upon time limit.
4. If a discussion is going nowhere, consider postponing further discussion on that question until you have taken care of other business.
5. If family members get bogged down in a discussion, the person in charge of the meeting may want to summarize the thinking and ask for possible solutions.

EXERCISE

Hold a family meeting to discuss the following questions:

1. What do you as an individual want to get out of your sports experiences?
2. What does our family want to get out of our sports experiences?
3. If there are differences, how can we resolve them?
4. How do sports fit with the other things that our family wants to accomplish?

5. When should family obligations take priority over sports obligations (and vice-versa)?

6. Do the sports programs we are currently involved in fit with what we are trying to achieve as a family? If not, what should we do about it?

Discussion:

As children get older, they tend to feel that their family is less important than their friends and activities. Those feelings can be difficult for a parent to understand, especially if you have made great sacrifices for which your children seem less than grateful. Before a family meeting, ask each member to draw a picture or diagram (such as a "pie chart") showing what they feel are the different components of a successful life. Compare and contrast drawings as you bring up the following points:

• A successful life includes having balance among family, friends, and others;

• Balance means that sometimes family will come first, and other times things like sports will come first.

SELF-ASSESSMENT

• How good are you at running a family meeting? If you were to ask your family for suggestions on ways to improve your family meetings, what might they say?

• Is your approach to leading family meetings helping other members of the family become effective decision makers? How can you help family members develop their group leadership skills?

• How clear are you, personally, about the role sports should play in your family life? Whom can you talk to who can help you clarify your thinking?

HOW TO INVOLVE MOMS AND DADS IN SPORTS DECISIONS

As Patrick and Alecia settle into the bleachers to watch Darren's game, they are greeted by Erv and Juanita, the parents of one of Darren's teammates. "Hey, that boy of yours is doing pretty good this year," Erv says. "He's a sure bet to make one of the select teams."

Alecia frowns. "I don't know if I like that idea. I think the kids on select get a little too blood thirsty, if you know what I mean. I don't think they have as much fun."

Patrick interrupts. "You know, Darren and I have done some talking about the possibility. I think it would solidify his chances for a scholarship, as well as sharpen his competitive skills. It would be too good to pass up."

What are some appropriate goals for the Hawkins family to set regarding their children's sports experiences? Who should determine these goals? If Patrick and Alecia have different opinions about the goals of youth sports, how should they resolve them?

LEARNING CONFLICT-RESOLUTION SKILLS

Family members in conflict need to:

- Listen to each other's point of view without put-down;
- Focus on only the situation at hand (no dragging up past history!);
- Try to understand the other person's point of view; and
- Arrive at win-win solutions.

Four basic steps to resolving conflict:

1. **Identify the problem.** In Patrick and Alecia's case, the problem is not that one is right and one is wrong. The problem is that because of their backgrounds, they view sports in two different ways, and eventually those ways are going to conflict.

2. **Generate solutions.** Come up with as many options as possible and write them down. Recognize that there is usually more than one way to resolve a problem. For example, one thing Patrick and Alecia might do is encourage Darren to seek advice from someone who has been in a similar situation and use that information to generate a solution.

3. **Evaluate and negotiate solutions.** This is where you weed out the good ideas from the bad and work toward a win-win solution. What points do you both agree on? What are you inflexible on? In what areas are you willing to give a little? In Darren's situation, one win-win solution might be for Darren to attend a summer sports camp at a college he likes. That would help him be seen by college coaches (Patrick's goal) while avoiding the cut throat atmosphere of a select team (Alecia's concern).

4. **Implement your solution.** Establish a game plan (the family meeting could be a good place to do this) and put it into action.

EXERCISE

To avoid conflicts down the line, take time to establish a family mission statement for sports. The statement should express your family's shared vision and values. Each family member, regardless of sports experience or background, should contribute to the mission statement and agree on the final result. When problems arise or choices need to be made, your mission statement can be used to remind you of what is most important to your family.

Discussion:

To start the brainstorming process, ask family members to think of as many words and/or phrases they can think of that would describe their ideal family sports experience. Which of these things does everyone agree is important? (You may want to refer back to your discussions in 1 and 2.)

Now, try putting these qualities into a statement that reflects what your family wants to get out of sports. Some suggested beginnings might be: "Our family's mission is to use sports to ..." "In our family, 'good' sports means ..." or "The family that plays together ..." Make sure that everyone has an equal voice in this process; no one person's ideas or suggestions should be seen as more important than anyone else's. In addition, remind everyone that a mission statement is not something that is etched in stone. They can be revisited and revised as situations within the family change. Make a habit as a family to review your sports mission statement at the beginning of each school year to see if it still reflects everyone's views.

SELF-ASSESSMENT

- Do you believe that the parent with the most sports experience should have the most say in family sports decisions? In what ways might another person's perspective be just as valuable?

- Do you ever unconsciously take the lead in sports discussions because of your greater experience (or defer to someone else because you have less experience)? What message do you think this sends to your children and to your partner?

- If your partner has little or no interest in sports, how can you and other family members demonstrate respect for that lack of interest while still including them in family sports discussions and decision making?

4

HOW TO LET YOUR CHILDREN'S SPORTS DREAMS BE THEIR OWN

Patrick comes home after watching one of Rochelle's soccer matches and says, "Guess what, Rochelle? Your coach told me about a great soccer camp this summer that could really help improve your skills! I told her to send me the paperwork. It's expensive, but this could really give you an edge in competition!"

Instead of acting excited, Rochelle pouts. "Dad, I already told Coach I wasn't interested in that camp. My friends and I have a lot of other things we want to do this summer."

Patrick turns to his wife for support. "Alecia...?"

"Well, dear," Alecia responds, "I don't want to send her if she's going to be miserable. They're not kids for very long, you know. Let her have fun."

Patrick and Rochelle obviously have different ideas about what level of commitment is appropriate in sports. What do you think they should do about it?

IMPROVING PARENT/CHILD COMMUNICATION SKILLS

Teenagers have a tendency to believe that their parents could not possibly understand them. To dispel this belief, you need to develop the ability to empathize with your children as they face sports-career decisions. Empathy means being able to see something from another person's point of view.

Developing empathy skills:

When we listen, most of us tend to respond in one of the following ways:
- We evaluate
- We probe
- We advise
- We interpret

All four types of responses are influenced by our own experiences and behavior, but none of them really helps us understand the other person. Empathy requires setting aside our feelings, beliefs, and experiences.

To listen with empathy to our children as they deal with their sports decisions, try rephrasing the content and reflecting the feeling behind what the other person is saying. For example: "Oh man, Mom, football sucks! I want to quit."

An evaluative response might be "Over my dead body! Do you know how much I paid for your equipment?"

An empathetic response might be "You're feeling frustrated with football? Tell me what you're finding so disappointing about it."

Once your child feels that you really understand his or her feelings, then she or he will be more open to your advice.

EXERCISE

As a family, pick one or both of the following role-play situations to practice your empathy skills:

1. Your child comes home from practice and says he or she wants to quit RIGHT NOW!

2. You want your child to try out for an elite team but she or he does not want to.

Discussion:

Take turns playing the role of child and parent. Doing so will not only help your child to see your point of view, but will give you better insight into the views of your child.

SELF-ASSESSMENT

- Under what circumstances are you best at listening to what your children are really trying to say?

- Under what circumstances are you not so good at listening to your children?   *Each week, pick a time when you make yourself available to listen to your children's reports on how things are going for them in their sports programs.   On those occasions refrain from any evaluative comments.   If they ask you to comment on their observations, redirect a question to them such as "Well, what do you think about it?"   Express your confidence in their ability to handle their own decisions.   Offer your thoughts at a time when you think your child will know that you have had an opportunity to think over his or her dilemma.   This delayed response procedure can prevent knee-jerk reactions ("Over my dead body."). Knee-jerk reactions come across to your children as insensitive, as you appear to be making a judgment without getting enough information about what your child might be experiencing. Such reactions also take decisions out of children's hands, taking away opportunities to help your children learn to take responsibility for their own decisions.*

HOW TO UNDERSTAND THE COMMITMENT REQUIRED BY THE COACH

"Your coach said WHAT?" asks Alecia, as Darren slouches at the kitchen table.

Sighing, Darren repeats his statement. "He said we won't win the championship unless we beat West High, and we won't beat West High unless we practice our butts off. So we have to attend practice during spring break, or we'll be benched."

"Well, that's ridiculous," says Alecia. "We've got our plane tickets and your dad has been looking forward to this vacation all year. There's no way you're staying home."

"Mom! This is the most important game of the year!" protests Darren. "I have to play!"

What should Patrick and Alecia do if they feel Darren's coach is making demands that interfere with Darren's participation in family functions?

ESTABLISHING A POSITIVE PARENT/COACH RELATIONSHIP

Successful coaches create, nurture, and maintain an environment that allows a positive relationship between coaches, athletes, and parents. But they cannot do so alone! You need to work with your children's coaches to increase the potential for enjoyment, personal growth, and success through sports.

Ways to keep the parent/coach interactions positive:

- Communicate clearly and openly. Meet with the coach at the beginning of the season. Together, you should discuss:
    - the demands of the sport;
    - the coach's philosophy and coaching style;
    - your family's sports philosophy;
    - how you can work together to achieve your mutual objectives.
- Encourage the coach (if he or she does not already) to put policies in writing and have parents and athletes indicate that they understand them.
- Follow the chain of command for parent/coach communication (speak with the coach before talking with the program administrator or the principal).
- Conduct yourself in a professional manner. Try not to take criticism of your child personally. Handle confrontations privately; never let encounters with the coach turn into arguments.

EXERCISE

Make a list of everything coaches have done in the past that have bothered or irritated you. Brainstorm ways you can prevent such actions from provoking a response that compromises your relationships with either the coach or your child.

Discussion:

Keep in mind that communication that happens early (perhaps even before the season begins) is likely to improve the chances that your family and the coach will have a positive relationship. Take advantage of opportunities to demonstrate that you support the team and the program as a whole, and you will find it easier to carry on a dialogue with your children's coaches. Remember, most parents are advocates for their own children, which is as it should be. The parents that make an impression on coaches are those who become advocates for the program, too.

SELF-ASSESSMENT

• What are your attitudes about coaches in general? *How do you think these attitudes are impacting the way you are relating to your children's specific coaches?*

• How good are you at getting into the coaches' heads? *List what you consider to be the major concerns of each of your children's coaches. Test out these ideas with someone who has had the experience of coaching. Anticipate how a coach with his or her priorities might structure their sports program. Try to anticipate the potential points of conflict that you might have with your children's coaches.*

• Under what circumstances might you lose your cool with a coach while observing a practice or a game? *Think through the various actions you might take when you see something you feel is not in your child's best interest.*

• Recognizing your strengths and limitations, under what circumstances would it be best for you to coach your child on how to directly address a point of conflict with the coach, and under what circumstances would it be appropriate for you to get involved on your child's behalf? *In both cases, it is essential that you get your child's "buy-off" on any action that is taken.*

HOW TO HELP YOUR CHILDREN BECOME ADVOCATES FOR THEIR INTERESTS

"Oh, man!" Rochelle groans. "I can't believe this!"

"What's the matter?" Alecia asks.

"I was just going over this play rehearsal schedule that we got today," Rochelle replies. "I thought it would all work out, but there are a half-dozen times that rehearsal will conflict with practice. And you know the coach's rule: You can only miss practice if you're sick or there's a family emergency. What am I going to do? I don't want to quit the team, but I don't want to quit the play, either! I've got a starring role!"

What can Alecia and Patrick do to help Rochelle participate in a variety of school activities?

TEACHING YOUR CHILDREN NEGOTIATING SKILLS

Negotiating is a skill that will help your child succeed in all aspects of life. A problem many people have with negotiating is that they come away feeling they have given away or lost too much. Making sure that both parties end up satisfied is the mark of a successful negotiator.

- Strategies you can teach your children to help them become more effective negotiators:

- Do their homework. Know what their position is, what the other person's position is, what concessions they're willing to make, and what things are not negotiable.

- Never demand. Instead, ask questions like, "I want to be a good member of the team—how can we work this out so that it works for both of us?"
- Never negotiate against themselves. Sometimes they are so eager to close the deal, they offer the other person more than he or she would have asked for.
- Know when to keep their mouths shut. A long silence can encourage the other person to offer more.
- Emphasize points of agreement. When they emphasize the things they agree on, it becomes easier to negotiate the things about which they disagree.
- Never give up. If they feel stuck, try the "if-then" approach. "If I can get the drama teacher to schedule my scenes for late in the rehearsal, would you let me leave practice a half-hour early?"

EXERCISE

Using the above scenario between Rochelle and her coach as an example, role play a negotiation between them. Be sure to include each of the "strategies for successful negotiating." Afterwards, evaluate the performance and discuss alternative ways of handling the situation.

Discussion:

During your evaluation of the performance, talk about what parts of the role play were difficult for your child. Doing so will help you identify areas for future practice sessions. Negotiation skills take some time to develop, so do not be surprised if your child has trouble with them at first. Be willing to practice role playing multiple times until your child begins to feel comfortable and confident.

SELF-ASSESSMENT

• Are you really open to accepting your child's choices? Would you be able to censor your reactions so that you do not show disappointment with your child's choice if it does not conform to what you would like him or her to do? At what point would it be appropriate for you to express your preference? *Consider the various ways you might offer your counsel. Also determine when is the best time in the decision-making process to offer your thoughts.*

• How effective are you as a negotiator? *Tell your child that you, too, are able to learn from participating in role-playing negotiating sessions.*

• Under what circumstances would it be appropriate for you to become the negotiator for your child? *Try not to let your children retreat from assuming responsibility for becoming advocates for their own interests, regardless of how persistent they are in insisting that you become their advocate.*

HOW TO HELP YOUR CHILDREN
LEAD BALANCED LIVES

"Patrick, I'm concerned," Alecia says one night. "Darren's friend Brad called tonight to see if Darren wanted to go hiking this Saturday, but Darren said no, he had practice. But Darren doesn't have practice this Saturday. Not a scheduled one, anyway. He's just going to spend most of the day in the gym, like he always does."

"I'm not understanding the problem here, Alecia."

"The problem is, everything is sports, sports, sports for Darren. I don't think it's good for him. He needs to take some time just to hang out with his friends."

"His grades aren't going down, are they?" Patrick asks. Alecia shakes her head. "Well, then, I wouldn't worry too much. As long as he's on track for a scholarship, he'll be fine."

How can Patrick and Alecia work together to help their children lead balanced lives?

UNDERSTANDING THE NEED FOR BALANCE

This need for balance is important not only in sports, but in all aspects of life. To help your children determine whether they are living balanced lives, ask them to examine the following areas of their lives and decide if they are giving enough attention to each:

- Family life
- Health/physical fitness
- Friendships
- Intellectual growth
- Emotional growth
- Spiritual development
- Finances/career development

EXERCISE

Have your children answer the following questions to help them determine whether they are spending too much time with sports.

1. Do you sit down to dinner with your family more than once a week?

2. Outside of school work, have you read more than four non-sports books in the last year?

3. When you read a newspaper, do you read any part other than the sports section?

4. Do you have more than two friends who are neither teammates nor athletes?

5. If you were unable to play sports for the next six months, would you have plenty of other activities to fill your time?

6. Is the majority of your television time spent watching sports?

If your children answered "yes" to four or more questions, congratulate them on working to keep well-balanced lives! If your children answered "no" to four or more questions, they need to think of ways they can better balance sports with other activities that are equally important.

Discussion:

If you want your sports-obsessed children to become engaged in other activities, it is important to understand what they find compelling about their sports experiences. Is it the excitement? The opportunity to compete? When you have determined what drives your children, it becomes easier to help them find other activities that allow them to live balanced lives. You can only learn of their interests by listening carefully to what they are telling you and observing closely the choices they make in their everyday lives. However, early exposure to a variety of activities is clearly the best way for children to find other activities that engage them.

SELF-ASSESSMENT

• Who are the people you most admire? How are sports positioned in their lives? *Before you can help your children live balanced lives, it is important that you have a clear image of what constitutes "the balanced life."*

• How balanced is your own life? *Think about your own answers to the* Exercise *questions. If you really want your children to live balanced lives, you need to model one yourself.*

HOW TO HELP YOUR CHILDREN
ASSESS THEIR INTERESTS

Rochelle's coach comes up to Patrick and Alecia after another one of Rochelle's excellent performances. "That's quite an athlete you have there," the coach says, as Patrick and Alecia beam. "I know Rochelle participates in several sports — has she thought about specializing?"

"No," Alecia says. "She enjoys all of her sports, and since she seems to be good at each one, we just let her do whatever she can handle."

"I understand that," the coach replies. "But the reality is, if you're thinking of scholarships, you should probably encourage Rochelle to go with the sport she's best at. Competition is fierce, you know."

How should Patrick and Alecia help Rochelle decide on how to respond to her coach's recommendation?

HELPING YOUR CHILDREN REALISTICALLY
EVALUATE THEIR ATHLETIC GIFTS

Since getting to know yourself—your strengths and weaknesses—is part of the process of maturing as a human being, you need to give your children an opportunity to get better acquainted with themselves. The better they know themselves, the better able they will be to make important decisions about how to handle such sports decisions as *whether* to specialize and *when* to specialize.

Discuss these questions with your children to help them become more aware of themselves as athletes:

• What are the things in sports you most like to do?

• What are your strengths and weaknesses as an athlete?

• When you have free time, which sport do you participate in?

• Does anything prevent you from doing the things in sports you value as often as you would like? If so, what?

• What are some things you could do to increase the amount of meaningful activity in your sports life?

• How good are you at dealing with competing demands for your time?

• How efficient are you in the use of your time?

EXERCISE

Have each active athlete in the family (parents as well as children) write down their own answers to the above questions. Next, ask them to answer the same questions, but instead of answering them for themselves, answer them for the other athletes in the family. (For example, on the fifth question, instead of writing, "the things that I could do ..." you would write, "the things that Dad could do ...")

Compare answers. How accurate have you been in judging other family members' preferences?

Discussion:

Keep in mind that each of us is not equally gifted as an athlete. When preparing observations about other members of the family, encourage everyone to be positive and encouraging. Make observations that will be understood as constructive and supportive rather than those that can be interpreted as negative and critical.

SELF-ASSESSMENT

• How much have you invested over the years in achieving a clear understanding of your own strengths and weaknesses in sports? *It is not realistic to expect your children to recognize their own strengths and weaknesses if their parents do not model a self-critical and self-disclosing style. In your children's presence, openly reflect upon your own strengths and weaknesses. Also share with them the tough choices you have faced or are facing in your life, acknowledging, of course, that you grew up in a different era. We do, indeed, live in an era of specialization, and we need to openly recognize that if we are to have credibility with our children, we must refrain from imposing what might be outdated standards to their situations.*

• How much emphasis, directly and indirectly, do you as a parent place upon your children earning athletic scholarships? What are your motives? *When parents communicate their desire for their children to earn athletic scholarships, they unwittingly place pressure on them that can cause them to specialize too early in sports that they do not genuinely enjoy. All too frequently, this results in early burnout.*

9

HOW TO TEACH YOUR CHILDREN
TO MAKE INFORMED DECISIONS

Alecia looks at her son's shining face across the table. "Can you believe it, Mom?" he asks. "Bill Jones wants me to come train at his academy! Bill Jones! I mean, he's the best!"

Alecia glances at her husband, who looks every bit as thrilled as his son. "Yes, Darren, I know it's a great honor," she says. "But don't you think this would be too disruptive, for you and for the family? After all, this academy is 2,000 miles away!"

Patrick shakes his head. "I think we should seriously consider it, Alecia. Sure, it would be expensive, but we could swing it. Lots of families do."

How do you think the family should decide whether or not Darren leaves home to train at a residential facility with elite athletes and coaches?

MAKING INFORMED DECISIONS

When it comes to making decisions about sports, as with other aspects of their lives, children and teenagers are easily swayed by their emotions. One of the most valuable skills a parent can teach is how to make informed decisions. Use your family meetings to make sports decisions that affect the family.

• Steps families can take in the decision-making process:

• Have goals. Having goals will help you in the decision-making process, because you can ask yourself, "If I do this, will it bring me closer to achieving my goals?"

- Do your homework. Research all the possibilities before you make a decision.

- List the pros and cons. What are all the ways that making or not making a decision could affect you and those around you? Can you live with the results of your decision if it turns out to be wrong? If you can't, then the risk is too big to take.

- Consider the timing. For example, maybe going to the sports academy would be a good thing for Darren, but doing so now would put his family in a financial bind. Perhaps he could put the academy off for a year, giving his family the time to save money.

EXERCISE

At your next family meeting, choose one of the following scenes (or make up your own) to practice your decision-making skills:

1. Mom or Dad has just been offered a great job with a bigger salary in another state. Do you move or do you stay?

2. Your teenager has been offered an exclusive summer internship at a prominent company; it is great experience, but it pays little and conflicts with his or her sports schedule. What do you do?

Discussion:

These scenarios provide another great opportunity for you and your children to switch roles. Role play the scenes first from your own roles, then switch roles with your children so that everyone is provided with a better understanding of the other's perspective.

SELF-ASSESSMENT

- How do you typically make major life decisions? How systematic have you been in making important decisions that affect your career? *Parents need to be candid with their children about the challenges they face in weighing the pros and cons of various life choice;s, even now. Children need to understand that making decisions about which aspects of one's life should be given highest priority is something that follows someone throughout his or her entire career. Today, nearly all young people are going to be provided many opportunities throughout their lives to evaluate the consequences of leaving one location or one job to take advantage of new job offers. By helping your children learn how to weigh various options, you will have given them a very special gift.*

- How successful has your approach to decision making been? How successful were you in making decisions when you were your as young as your children? *It is sometimes valuable to reflect on your own pattern of development to help you remember what a long-term process it is to develop effective decision-making strategies.*

- Does your approach to decision making fit with your children's personal styles? *Some children are very intuitive in their approach to making decisions, while others are more systematic. We need to honor both approaches to making life decisions.*

- Should you teach your children *your* tested method of making career choices, or is there a method that would be a better fit for them? *Surely, you should share with your children the strategies you have determined fit with your personality, but you need to invite them to remain open to finding an approach that works better for them.*

- How involved do you need to be in your children's sports career decision making? *It is important to find a middle ground between dictating to your children the choices they need to make and leaving them to their own devices. Ultimately, your children need to be urged to take possession of the choices they make if they are to progress to the next level of development.*

10

HOW TO HELP YOUR CHILDREN DEAL WITH ADVERSITY

"Patrick! Did you see that? Oh, I think Darren's hurt!" Alecia clutches her husband's arm as they watch their son lie prone on the field.

"Come on, Darren, get up!" Patrick mutters to himself. With the help of his coach, Darren finally stands, but he limps badly as he leaves the field. Patrick and Alecia can see the pain etched across their son's face.

A few minutes later, as the game ends, they make their way over to where Darren is sitting.

"It looks like a bad sprain," the team's trainer informs them. "But you should have it X-rayed to make sure. Either way, Darren's out for several weeks at least, and maybe the rest of the season."

What can Patrick and Alecia do to prepare their children for the physical and psychological "bruises" that typically come with playing sports? How should Patrick and Alecia react when their children experience injuries or setbacks?

DEVELOPING EMOTIONALLY RESILIENT ATHLETES

Playing sports can bring a lot of stress into a child's life — stress that comes with not being chosen, with losing an important game, with being injured or hurt. You can help your children deal with these and other life stressors by helping them develop the kind of emotional resiliency that allows them to bounce back from disappointment and adversity. Research shows that children who are more resilient make better decisions and engage in less risky behavior. How do you build resilient young athletes?

- Help them develop a sense of self-efficacy (the belief that if they work hard at something, they can achieve it).

- Provide them with a supportive family. Olympic speed skater Dan Jansen often noted how important his family's support was in his quest to finally achieve a gold medal.

- Assure that they have a good relationship with at least one parent. This means spending one-on-one time, not just family time, with your children. Spending individual time with your children allows you to really connect with them, share experiences, and show how you have managed to overcome obstacles in your life.

- Encourage your children to establish important relationships with other adults. These mentors can reinforce the lessons and values that parents provide.

EXERCISE

To help your children conclude that they can meet any challenges that may come their way, discuss with them something (in sports, school, or other) that they would really like to master. Working together, develop game plans for achieving their announced goals.

Discussion:

Try to set up some specific achievable goals, as well as develop a specific plan for achieving them. For example, you might begin helping your children set the long-term goal of staying focused on the task at hand, avoiding distractions that keep them from giving everything they have. To achieve that goal, invite them to set smaller goals as stepping stones that can help them achieve the long-term goal. Your daughter might decide, for example, that during her next practice, she will stay completely focused on everything that the coach is asking for the first 10 minutes, consciously telling herself to "STOP" when a distraction arises. She might try each week to extend the amount of time she stays focused until remaining focused for the entire practice comes naturally. By setting a series of realistic, achievable short-term goals, your children will experience the kind of success that keeps them motivated to pursue them for the long-term, without becoming dispirited when they "hit a bump in the road."

SELF-ASSESSMENT

• How do you typically cope with adversity? *Reflect on adverse situations you have encountered in sports or in other aspects of your life. Do you detect a pattern? Are you typically stoic, or do you openly show your pain and frustration? Is your pattern one you want your children to follow? Does your approach fit with their personal styles of coping with the world? Are you using your own experience as a model for your children to follow? Is it realistic that your pattern will work for them?*

• Do you typically set clear goals for yourself in your sports life? *If you do not model a goal-setting approach that leads you to seek feedback about how successful you have been, it is highly unlikely that your children will be able to develop a "can-do" attitude that will allow them to cope effectively with setbacks.*

• What steps have you taken to prevent your children from adopting an approach promoted by many coaches that encourages them to "play through" pain, sometimes at the risk of doing permanent damage to themselves? *Being tough and being sensible are not always compatible. Parents are responsible for helping their children learn how to proceed intelligently when their bodies are telling them "no." The culture of sports demands that athletes not let a little pain prevent them from fulfilling their responsibilities to their teams. If parents do not help their children learn to obey signals from their bodies, without, of course, pampering themselves, it is likely that no one else will.*

11

HOW TO ASSESS YOUR KNOWLEDGE OF YOUR CHILDREN'S SPORTS

Darren and Patrick are in the living room, carefully watching a basketball game.

"Who's playing?" Alecia asks, as she walks into the room.

"This is the tape of our team playing last year's champs," Darren responds. "Our team's going into a zone. I want to see if the other guys match it."

"A zone?" Alecia asks. "I know I've heard the word, but what does it mean?"

Darren is happy to share his knowledge. "A zone is when you take responsibility for covering an area, rather than covering a man."

"Why would you want to do that?" Alecia asks. "I don't get it."

"Darren, you can't expect your mother to understand basketball," Patrick interrupts. "I remember back in my senior year when we tried the same kind of defense that your team is doing here. It was a mistake then, and it's a mistake now...." Darren cringes as Patrick begins another of his long-winded stories that allows him to demonstrate to his family just how much he knows — or used to know — about sports.

What can Alecia do to learn more about Darren's sport? How might Patrick's "know-it-all" attitude about sports affect his relationship with Darren and Darren's enthusiasm for the game?

BECOMING A STUDENT OF YOUR CHILDREN'S SPORTS

Often, parents have not had very much direct experience with their children's sports. Many moms have not had opportunities to develop sports skills and interests, and many of today's dads have not had much experience with the sports that are capturing the interest of their children (i.e., soccer, volleyball, and hockey). To demonstrate your commitment to your children's sports involvement, it is important for you to learn enough about their sports to share in their enjoyment. Doing so not only helps strengthen your bonds with your children, it also allows your children to see you modeling a continuing interest in learning new things.

Steps to Learning About Your Children's Sports

1. Let your children know you genuinely want to learn more about their sports. You can do that by sharing specific goals you have set for yourself. For example, you might say, "I want to understand the signals that the referee makes."

2. Demonstrate your interest through such activities as practicing basic sports skills, reading about the history of the sport, and/or by watching competitions with your child or a knowledgeable friend.

3. Test your knowledge by asking your children to quiz you about what you've learned.

4. Attend your children's practices. Do not hesitate to ask the coach to help you better understand the fine points of the game. You may want to suggest to the coach that she or he provide a sports orientation for parents at the beginning of the season.

5. Take care not to upstage your children by showing off your knowledge or skills. Keep in mind your original goal—to share the enjoyment of sports with your children.

EXERCISE

As a family, designate one week at the beginning of each sports season as "(Fill in the sport) Learning Week." Each person is assigned to
learn at least one new thing about that particular sport and share it
with the family that evening at dinner time.

Discussion:

Ask your children to begin by reporting what they have learned. Share what
you have learned with them — not just the knowledge you have gained, but
also the joy you are experiencing through learning and mastery of new sport.

SELF-ASSESSMENT

• Do you truly have a desire to learn more about your children's sports, or
do sports seem boring or uninteresting to you?

• Are there things about your early experiences with sports that have turned
you off to wanting to learn more about sports? How might reviewing
your personal sports history help you to overcome your resistance to
learning more about the subject?

• Do you feel resentful about the time it will take to invest in learning about
your children's sports? What are all the "positives" that would result
from taking the time to learn? Are these worth it to you?

• Do you feel that the sports knowledge you already have is more than
sufficient? Would you consider yourself a sports "expert"? How open
are you to the fact that there might still be things you could learn?

HOW TO REVISIT YOUR
CHILDHOOD SPORTS EXPERIENCES

Alecia catches Patrick going through some old scrapbooks. He is smiling at some clippings that show him as a high school athlete, winning the "Most Valuable Player" award.

"Man, I was pretty good back then," Patrick reminisces. "Just like Darren. You know, I bet he could easily win MVP this year, if he just put a little more effort into it."

"You weren't exactly like Darren," Alecia reminds him. "Darren has a life. If I remember correctly, you poured every waking minute into sports. The only date you ever had in school was with me, and that's only because my brother threatened to beat you up if you didn't."

Patrick frowns. "I didn't spend 'every waking minute' on sports."

"You did, too!" Alecia argues. "Patrick, if they'd had the same kind of academic standards that they do now, you never would have graduated!"

What can Patrick do to get an accurate picture of his youth sports experiences? How can revisiting his sports past help Patrick interact with Darren?

CAPTURING YOUR SPORTS HISTORY

As we all know, childhood plays an important role in shaping who you are and what you want out of life. Therefore, it will be helpful for you to take the time to put together an accurate history of your sports experiences, not only to better understand yourself, but also to better understand how you feel about your children's sports careers.

Things to Talk About in Your Sports "Biography"

- What sports you played, when and where
- Coaches and teammates
- Personal and team accomplishments
- Why you chose the sports you did
- Why you dropped out or continued playing
- Highs and lows
- Family sports experiences
- What you liked/hated about sports
- Things you learned from sports
- Etc., etc., etc.!

EXERCISE

The idea of sitting down and writing a history is daunting to many people. Make the task easier and more enjoyable by breaking it into pieces. Each week, choose one of the above "biography" topics and write a delightful remembrance to share with your family! Another approach is to do something other than writing. Make your history visual by drawing or clipping images from magazines and newspapers that match your history. Or consider recording it on an audio or video tape. The important thing is to capture your history as accurately as possible, so if writing is something that comes hard to you, think of another way to capture that history.

Discussion:

What are some of the defining moments in your sports career — moments when a person or an event affected the choices you made to either continue or drop out of a particular sports activity? Talk about some of these moments with your children. Share with them why you think a particular event or interaction stayed with you so long and how these experiences have affected how you've approached sports throughout your life.

SELF-ASSESSMENT

- How essential an ingredient have sports been in your life?
- If you drew circles that represented the various roles you play (for example, parent, child, spouse, worker, church member, etc.), how big would the athlete/sports fan circle be in relation to the others?
- Does the importance (or lack of importance) that you have placed on sports in your life affect the advice you give your children as they move through their sports careers? Is there anything you can do to ensure that the advice you give is balanced?

HOW TO LOOK AT SPORTS
THROUGH YOUR CHILDREN'S EYES

Alecia has gone with her sister to watch her 10-year-old nephew's Little League game. Alecia likes watching Alex play because, win or lose (and his team loses a lot), he always has a good time. This time, however, she is surprised to see her nephew looking sad.

"What's the matter with Alex?" Alecia asks her sister.

"Oh, he's sulking," her sister replies. "His dad wants him to try out for the Stars (an elite team across town), but Alex says he won't have fun if he can't play with his friends. Alex is a good player, Alecia — don't you think he'd enjoy being on a good team once he got used to it?"

What role might Alex's parents be playing in this problem? What can Alecia do to help her sister look at the situation from Alex's perspective?

UNDERSTANDING INDIVIDUAL EXPECTATIONS

The majority of family problems regarding sports could be easily overcome if family members simply understood one another better. One way to gain this understanding is to have a clear idea of what each family member's expectations are when it comes to sports. For example, for a young child like Alex, sports are mostly a time to have fun with friends. Older children, on the other hand, often use sports as a way to be popular. In the meantime, parents see sports as a way to provide scholarships and honors for their children. How can you tell if your expectations are influencing how you view your children's sports experiences?

Understanding Your Expectations

• How satisfied you are with something (sports, life, etc.) depends on how much your expectations are being met. If you are feeling dissatisfied with how your child is doing in sports, it could be a sign that your expectations are unrealistic or need to be adjusted.

• Your expectations influence how you judge people. If you expect your child to act in a certain way (for example, expecting a six-year-old to stay sharply focused during every moment of a competition), then you may judge them harshly when those expectations aren't met. You need to ask yourself: "Are my expectations realistic? Do I know what my child's expectations for the sport are? How can I better understand the situation so I can see if there's a need to adjust my expectations?"

EXERCISE

On a piece of paper, have your children list their top three reasons for wanting to play sports. While they are writing, make your own list of what you think their top three reasons are going to be. Compare the lists. How closely do they match? Now repeat the exercise, only with the children listing what they think are the parent's top three reasons for wanting their children to play sports, and vice-versa.

Discussion:

What do the above lists show about how well you and your children understand each other's expectations when it comes to sports? What are some things you could do as a family that would help you to view sports and other things through one another's perspectives? Whose views should be most important—those of you or your child?

SELF-ASSESSMENT

• Would you say that, overall, your children wish you understood them better, or do they feel that you understand them too well?

• Generally, how good are you at figuring out the reasons behind the sports decisions your children make?

• Do you meet regularly (and individually) with your children to discuss how they feel about their sports involvement? If you answered "no," why not?

• Have you ever asked your children to share their sports dreams with you? If you do ask, are your children hesitant? Why or why not?

HOW TO LEARN TO COPE WITH FRUSTRATION

"C'mon, Rochelle! Dive for the ball! Get it! Get it!" Patrick groans as he watches his daughter blow a chance at a score. Turning to Alecia, he complains, "You know, if Rochelle doesn't start scoring more, she'll never be able to play at the college level. I don't know what that coach thinks she's teaching those girls. Doesn't she know they'll never win at anything if they don't play with more intensity? I don't know, maybe I'm expecting too much." He breaks off suddenly when he sees the coach pull Rochelle from the game. "Hey! Hey! What are you doing, you idiot!!" Patrick shouts, while his wife cringes in embarrassment. "How do you expect her to learn anything if she's not playing!!"

How might Patrick's outbursts negatively affect his family? What should Patrick do to cope with his frustration in a way that avoids such an effect?

KNOWING HOW TO KEEP YOUR COOL

It's virtually impossible to avoid feeling frustrated — especially in an emotionally charged sports setting. However, while you can't control the feeling, you CAN refuse to nourish it, and you can control how you behave in response to the feeling.

Five Ways to Think Before You Act

1. Be honest and realistic about your children's motivations, interests, abilities, and needs.
2. Be committed to placing your children's interests and needs above your own.
3. Recognize that feelings and behaviors are two different things.
4. Accept responsibility for how you behave (don't blame it on your children, the coaches, the referees, or anyone else).
5. Recognize what things trigger frustration in you and develop a coping strategy (e.g., if you get frustrated when games are close, maybe you need to take a walk at those times).

EXERCISE

Perform a cost/benefit analysis of your behavior when you get frustrated at sporting events, weighing the costs of giving into frustration against the benefits of freely venting your feelings. Some questions to consider: How do people around you react when you show frustration? How do you think your expressions of frustration affect your children, their teammates, the coaches, and other parents? What kind of image do you project when you "lose your cool" at games?

Discussion:

Get input from your family on how they feel your behavior is affecting them and others in the sports community. Ask them how they view your conduct and what suggestions they have to help you behave in a more positive way.

SELF-ASSESSMENT

• What frustrates you about watching your children compete? Why do you think you feel frustrated in these situations? Do you:

- Consider your children extensions of yourself and feel embarrassed when they don't perform well?

- Think the coaches have not adequately prepared your children?

- Feel a loss of control over the situation?

- Think your children are not paying attention to the coaches?

- Fear that your children are not talented enough?

- Feel that the other athletes on the team are not giving your children opportunities to perform?

• Have you ever tried to focus on aspects of sports other than how well your children are doing? (For example, the sportsmanship exhibited by the teams, the chance to establish friendships with other parents, the graceful movements of the athletes?) How might focusing on some of these things help you better control your frustration?

HOW TO DISCOVER
NEW PERSPECTIVES ON SPORTS

As Patrick and Alecia watch Rochelle's team run onto the field, Patrick is suddenly struck by the big smiles on the faces of the girls. "Hey, Alecia," he says, "have you ever noticed that when the girls come out to play, they always look happy, but when Darren and his teammates come running out, it's like a contest to see who can look the meanest?"

Patrick's comments are interrupted by a loud burst of laughter from the field. "That's another thing I've noticed," Patrick continues. "The girls just seem to have more fun when they're playing. They're more considerate of each other, too. I like that."

"Maybe you should try it some time," Alecia says. "You talk about Darren, but have you ever seen yourself compete? You have a pretty 'mean' face, too."

What can today's women teach parents — especially fathers — about sports and life? How might broadening his perspective help Patrick enjoy sports more?

BROADENING YOUR PERSPECTIVE

As a parent, you need to be able to recognize when your usual approach to sports isn't reaping the maximum benefit for you or your children. (Acknowledging one's limitation in one's approach to sports can be especially difficult for dads, for whom "traditional" ways of thinking about sports have most likely been ingrained since childhood.) What can you do to open yourself to new ways of looking at sports?

- Be willing to feel uncomfortable. If you've spent many years thinking about sports as a battle for dominance, trying to change your mental set will probably be challenging. If you expect to feel some uneasiness when you are making a change, you will be more likely to be able to take the decisive actions that will allow you to change.

- Be willing to keep going. Whenever you are trying to change a long-held belief or way of thinking about something, you need to give your new approach a fair test. If you were trying to learn a new sports skill, you wouldn't expect to learn it overnight, would you? (Pitchers in baseball know that learning to throw a knuckleball can take years to perfect!) It's the same with trying to change your patterns of thinking.

- Be patient. There may be times you will get discouraged because no one else seems to share your new perspective. For example, a father might find that the other dads kid him about "going soft," or a mother who's fighting for equal sports opportunities for her daughters might encounter resistance from other moms who think she's too militant. Try to find someone to talk to who is not as tied to traditional ways of appreciating sports.

EXERCISE

Record a televised sports competition. As a family, listen to a segment of the broadcast and write down all the words and phrases the commentators use that paint a picture of sports as a "battle" that only the valiant will win. Replay the action without the sound and write a new script that emphasizes the beauty and grace of athletic performance. (You could either write one script as a family, divide into teams, or have each family member write his or her own script.) Then play the recording again, using your script(s) in place of the televised one.

Discussion:

Did describing the sports action with new words and images change the way family members felt about what was happening on the playing field? How might regularly looking at sports in this new way benefit your family?

SELF-ASSESSMENT

• How much of a sports "traditionalist" are you? What aspects of your childhood and youth contributed to the way you view sports?

• What is the most difficult change you have ever had to make in your sports thinking? (e.g., accepting that girls can be just as skilled as boys; believing that winning isn't everything, etc.) What were the most difficult barriers you had to overcome in making that change? Why do you think these barriers were so difficult for you?

• How do you feel about change in general? Do you like new challenges and risks? Do you dislike them but forge ahead because you know you must? Or do you avoid change as much as possible?

• If your previous experiences with change suggest that adding new dimensions to your current perspective on sports might be difficult, what can you do about that?

• What values and/or interests do you have that could be helpful to you as you try to expand your range of sports experiences?

HOW TO HELP YOUR CHILDREN OVERCOME GENDER-ROLE STEREOTYPES IN SPORTS

Rochelle is quite angry when she arrives home from school one day. "Those stupid boys!" she exclaims to her mother. "Do you know what I heard them saying today?"

"What boys?" Alecia asks.

"Some of the football players," Rochelle says. "They were talking about Mary and Jill. You know — Mary was the one who won the state championship last year in cross-country? Anyway, the guys were complaining because they'd gotten into a big argument with Mary and Jill about training and conditioning — and of course, the girls were right. So the guys said, and I quote, 'Girl jocks are just a bunch of bitches. If you want to find a real woman, you have to date a cheerleader.'"

How can Alecia help Rochelle recognize and overcome the influences of gender-role stereotyping in sports?

CHANGING INGRAINED ATTITUDES ABOUT SPORTS AND GENDER

Attitudes are hard to change — especially those that have been ingrained over the course of centuries. The prevailing attitude has been that sports are primarily a masculine pursuit, and the more successful you are, the more "masculine" you are. Is it any wonder, then, that girls who enjoy and are successful at sports are perceived as being "masculine," and boys who don't enjoy sports or aren't good at them are seen as less than masculine? What can parents do to challenge these attitudes and replace them with more positive ones?

- Read about attitudes regarding men, women, and sports or talk about these attitudes with coaches, sports administrators, or teachers, then discus what you have learned with your children.
- Identify and celebrate positive sports role models of both genders (e.g., the professional football player who took time off to care for his children while his wife battled cancer, or the first female referees in the NBA).
- Point out to your children the attitudes you learned as a child; discuss how they influence your behavior as a sports parent. Be honest.
- Discuss with your children how their own words and actions reflect current stereotypes about men and women in sports.

EXERCISE

As a fun way of pointing out how silly some of our ingrained attitudes are, have your family do a talk show parody. Pick a title (for example, "Jocks Who Cry and the Women Who Love Them!" or "My Mother Can Bench-Press Your Mother!") and assign the roles of moderator, guests, and audience members (if you have enough people). You may want to videotape your production.

Discussion:

Did the above activity raise any questions for your family about the consequences of believing such gender-role stereotypes as "boys don't cry" and "girls can't be tough"? How did participating in this activity cause your family to re-think some of its attitudes towards girls, boys, and sports?

SELF-ASSESSMENT

• To what extent do you still harbor traditional gender-role sports stereo-types? For example, do you maintain the same expectations for your daughter as you do for your son? In your daily interactions with your children, do you unknowingly support old-fashioned stereotypes? (For instance, is it automatically assumed that girls do the housework while the boys take care of the yard and the car?)

• How do you address the issue that the male body is generally better equipped to perform in sports requiring strength and speed? Does this make a difference in how you should treat your son versus how you treat your daughter? Does this affect how you approach sports with your son versus how you approach sports with your daughter?

• How do you address the issue that women typically have a different emotional makeup and are generally less interested in confrontation and conflict on the playing field? Has this difference (which coaches some-times refer to as "mental toughness") affected how you treat your son versus how you treat your daughter?

• Do you feel that one approach (mental toughness versus caring and consideration) is better than the other, or would you prefer that your children have all of these qualities on the playing field?

17

HOW TO HELP YOUR CHILDREN DEAL WITH AN OVERLY ZEALOUS COACH

At dinner one night, Rochelle mentions that two of her teammates quit the team that day. "Two more?" Alecia asks. "Was it because of the coach again?" Rochelle nods. It is no secret that her coach is a real taskmaster. Already, several candidates for the team have been unable to survive his coaching techniques. "That does it!" Alecia says. "I think you should transfer to a club with a different coach — one who treats players with more respect."

Patrick shakes his head. "No, I don't think that's a good idea. Sure, he's tough, but he helps the girls become better competitors. And if Rochelle can get along with him, she can get along with anyone. What do you think, Rochelle?"

"I don't know. Sometimes he makes me so mad I just want to quit. But I know he pushes me to become a better player. Maybe I should just suck it up and stick with the team."

How can Patrick and Alecia best support Rochelle in this situation? How can they help her learn to effectively manage her relationship with a difficult coach without getting hurt in the process?

DEALING WITH A DIFFICULT COACH

Sooner or later, your children will run into people who are difficult, whether it's a coach, a teacher, or an employer. You can perform an incredibly valuable service for your children by helping them develop effective strategies for dealing with these kinds of leaders.

Advice You Can Give Children with Difficult Coaches:

- Try to understand the reasons behind the coach's behavior. Has the coach achieved success in the past by coaching this way? Is the coach motivated by genuine concern for the athletes or by a desire to win? Is the coach experiencing personal or professional problems that are affecting his or her behavior?

- Stand up for yourself. When you stand up straight and look your coach in the eye, you send the message that you deserve respect.

- If you decide to speak to your coach, pick a time when you are both calm. Do not be overly hostile or aggressive (e.g., "I hate it when you yell at me!"). Calmly explain that while the coach's methods may be effective with some people, you do not feel they're helping you reach your potential.

- Give yourself the option of quitting. Sometimes, just knowing that you can walk away at any time gives you the ability to see it through.

- Think about the pros and cons of both sticking with and leaving this team. Decide what will serve you best in your life interests, make a decision, then feel good about it. If you see it through with this team, don't take things personally; instead, remind yourself that your stay on the team is temporary and learn what you can from being there.

EXERCISE

With your child, role play a situation where he or she talks to the coach about the difficult behavior. Take turns playing both roles. Play the scene more than one way. For example, the first time you could have the coach respond defensively. Then you could have the coach ignore the issues the athlete presents. Finally, you could have the coach respond attentively but refuse to consider changing his or her behavior.

Discussion:

After each script has been played out, ask your child how he or she felt about the way the coach responded. Make sure your child has an answer prepared in case the coach asks something like: "How would you want me to act when I see you not giving your full effort or making unnecessary mistakes?" Discuss ways your child can state the problem without making the coach feel like he or she is under attack.

SELF-ASSESSMENT

• Do you automatically accept the picture your child paints about his or her "difficult" coach, or do you observe practices and games and talk to other parents so you can better evaluate the situation?

• Did you have any experiences with difficult coaches when you were young? How might your experience influence the advice you give your children?

• Do you feel you have the knowledge and/or experience to know the difference between a demanding coach and an abusive coach? How much over zealous coaching are you willing to tolerate before advising your child to quit the team or give you permission to express your concerns to the coach or to his or her supervisor?

• If your child did want you to talk to the coach, would you be able to do so calmly? What things might cause you to lose your temper? What could you do in advance to avoid doing so?

HOW TO HELP YOUR CHILDREN ACHIEVE A BALANCE BETWEEN BEING SUCCESSFUL AND BEING A *GOOD* FRIEND

After school, Rochelle calmly tells her mother, "Don't tell Dad, but I've decided to switch teams this year. I want to play on Cindy's team instead."

Alecia is very surprised. The team Rochelle has been on is one of the best in the area, and Rochelle has been a key to its success. Trying not to betray her disappointment, Alecia replies, "What made you decide that?"

"Lots of things. Like, Cindy's one of my best friends, and so are Kylie and Trish, and they're all on that team together. They have so much fun, too! And they all really, really want me to be with them."

"Have you talked to your coach about this?" Alecia asks.

"No, that will be tough," Rochelle admits. "I know he'll be upset."

"Your dad probably will be, too," Alecia replies. "We'll have to talk about it when he gets home," she concludes, hoping that Patrick will be able to talk some sense into Rochelle.

What approach should the Hawkinses take in response to Rochelle's decision? What options do they have? What are the costs and benefits of each option?

HELPING YOUR CHILDREN SET PRIORITIES

We're always in the position of having to choose one thing over another, and with those choices come a sense of loss for the thing we didn't choose. To avoid that feeling of loss, we often put off making the decision, try to get some-one else to make it for us, or scramble desperately to figure out how we can "have our cake and eat it, too." You need to help your children realize that making those difficult decisions will be easier—and more beneficial—if they have a clear understanding of their priorities in life and in sports. The key for your children is not that they prioritize everything on their schedule. Rather, with your help, they need to learn to schedule their priorities — that is, to take charge of their lives in ways that give them the opportunity to meet their needs and fulfill their dreams. You can help your children learn to schedule their priorities by:

- Helping them understand what values are important to them (e.g., relation-ships may be more important than athletic achievement to some; for oth-ers, it might be the opposite).
- Encouraging them to create a personal mission statement.
- Teaching them how to set clear, achievable goals.

EXERCISE

Ask your children to write a personal mission statement that reflects what they want to be and do in life and how sports will help them accomplish that mission. Read the mission statement together and discuss how it might influence choices they have to make along the path to achieving their athletic dreams.

Discussion:

Discuss with your children the differences between their mission (their over-all goal in life), their vision (where they see themselves ending up in the next few years), their goals (specific things they wish to accomplish), and their ob-jectives (the things they need to start doing in order to achieve their goals and accomplish their mission). Talk about different things they might want to in-clude in their mission statement; give them some sample mission statements to help them think of ideas (such as your own personal mission statement or a company mission statement).

SELF-ASSESSMENT

• How effective are you in getting your children to set aside time to work with you on making important decisions about their athletic careers? Do you have a history of working closely with your children when they are facing such decisions?

• Do you think your children trust you to let them make their own decisions? How do you show that trust?

• How effective have you been in balancing your need to "stand out" with your need to be "part of the group"? Does one or the other usually take precedence for you? If so, why?

• How good are you at preparing a mission statement and using it to recognize and follow your priorities? Would you be willing to make creating and updating your mission statements a joint project with your children?

• When you were your children's ages, how effective were you at defining your life goals and developing a strategy for achieving them? Do you ever have difficulty choosing one activity over another? How do you resolve the problem?

HOW TO HELP YOUR CHILDREN CONTROL THEIR TEMPERS

Alecia can hardly believe her eyes as she watches Darren swing his elbow — hard — into the face of his opponent.

"Patrick, I think he did that on purpose!" Alecia exclaims. Apparently, the referee agrees, as he whistles Darren for a penalty. Outraged, Darren begins arguing with the ref, who promptly throws him out of the game.

"That's the second time this year that's happened," says Alecia. "Why is Darren acting like that?"

What steps should the Hawkinses take to help Darren learn to control his temper?

STAYING IN CONTROL

Strong emotions are a natural part of sports, but parents need to help their children understand that the best athletes use their emotions constructively. As a parent, what can you do to help your children recognize and rewire their "hot buttons"?

- Encourage them to become more aware of how they act when they lose control. For example, the next time they lose their tempers in a family setting, ask them:

- What are you thinking right now?

- What are your feelings at this moment? Do you like feeling this way?

- How would you rather feel?

- Do you think your actions are appropriate for this situation? What might be a more appropriate way of acting?

• Help your children to identify any irrational thoughts that might be contributing to their lack of control. Some of these irrational thoughts might include:

- "I'd better not fail. If I do, it's terrible."

- "The official hates me."

- "If I worry enough, things will work out better."

• Show your children how substituting a new thought ("If I argue this foul too much, I'll get thrown out of the game and that won't help my team") for the irrational one can help them stay in control.

EXERCISE

Have family members take turns sharing experiences in sports—or in other life situations—when their buttons were pushed and they reacted inappropriately. Ask each person to answer the following: What were your feelings/actions at the time? What kinds of irrational thoughts were you having? What thoughts did you substitute (or might you have substituted) to change your thinking?

Discussion:

It is important to help your children understand that anger and aggression are natural outcomes in competitive situations where a person's ego is being put on the line. At the same time, you need to point out that when they express anger and aggression in a way that interferes with the competition or spoils the experience for others, they are breaking an unspoken contract with their teammates and opponents to play the game safely, fairly, and the best they possibly can.

SELF-ASSESSMENT

• What kind of a model for controlling anger do you present to your children? Are you someone who tends to remain in control, or are you easily provoked?

• What kind of athletes do you most admire — the ones who seldom lose their tempers, or the ones who are always collecting fouls for their bad behavior? Why do you admire these athletes?

• When you compete (or competed) in sports, what are (or were) your "hot buttons"? What tactics do you use to keep from doing something you might regret when your buttons are pushed? Do you and your children share similar hot buttons? Do you think your methods for staying in control would work for them?

HOW TO HELP YOUR CHILDREN REALISTICALLY ASSESS THEIR OWN PERFORMANCES

"Boy, I am such a screw-up," complains Darren, after a game in which he played below his standard. "Coach will probably bench me next game."

"Oh, come on, Darren," says Patrick, trying to reassure him. "You had one off game. You're a great player!"

"Great players don't mess up like I did," responds Darren. "The other team probably won just because of me. I bet everyone was sitting there, thinking, 'Wow, that kid is really stupid!'"

What should the Hawkins family do when their children exaggerate the negative aspects of their performances?

CONDUCTING A PERFORMANCE APPRAISAL

When it comes to sports, it's sometimes hard for parents to be objective about their children's performances. That's why, when a child says, "I really stunk up the field today," a parent's natural response is often to respond, "Don't be silly — you were great!" However, for you and your children to evaluate the progress they are making toward their goals, it is necessary for you and them to know how to appraise their performances clearly and objectively. To do so:

- Make sure you know what the appropriate skill levels are for your children. For example, eight-year-olds should not be expected to do things that twelve-year-olds can.

- Understand that even within age groups, every child matures and develops differently. For example, is one of your children an agile, quick learner, while another is someone who needs to practice a skill over and over before getting it down?

- Work with your children to determine the best way of gathering information about their abilities. Here are three ways to do so:

  1. Talk to an impartial observer, such as a coach or older athlete who can give your children feedback on their performances.

  2. Keep a daily log. A daily log gives children specific and immediate feedback on their performances. For example, a runner might keep a daily log of distances run, types of courses (hills, track, etc.), times, and so on. Including comments about how the child felt each time and why a given performance might have stood out as better or worse than usual can also provide some valuable information about what kinds of things have a positive or negative effect on performance.

  3. Keep a checklist. The checklist method lists several items (as many as 10-20) of specific performance criteria. Children can take a few minutes each week to assess their own performances on each of the basic skills required in their sports (passing, dribbling, etc). You should urge your children to celebrate each time they reach a new level of accomplishment. For example, if one child has been making 6 out of 10 free throws in practice and now hits 7 out of 10, it is time to celebrate. Focusing on skills rather than the score gives your children more opportunities to be uplifted by their sports experiences.

EXERCISE

Have each child choose a method of performance appraisal. Determine how often they will conduct the appraisal (e.g., post a checklist by their bed; set up an interview with their coach).

Discussion:

After your children have been regularly assessing their progress for several weeks, discuss how having objective feedback has helped them improve their performances. Ask them if they can think of other areas of their lives where it would be helpful for them to start doing performance appraisals.

SELF-ASSESSMENT

- When you are competing, which matters more to you: that you improve your personal performance, or that you win? Which attitude do you model for your children? Which attitude do you want to model for your children?

- Do you make the effort to celebrate small steps toward achieving your personal sports goals? How might doing so benefit you?

- Are you willing to spend time working with your children as they try to broaden their sports skills? Are you confident that you can teach them what the coach wants them to learn?

HOW TO HELP YOUR CHILDREN
TAKE RESPONSIBILITY FOR SETBACKS

"You're right, Dad," says Darren. "It really wasn't my fault I had a bad game. Did you see some of those calls the officials were making? No wonder I couldn't get a break!"

"Well, actually..." Patrick begins.

"And Number 21 on their team!" Darren interrupts. "Did you see how many times he held on to my jersey?"

"But —"

Darren continues. "And of course, it didn't help any when Coach changed our offense right in the middle of everything. That really threw my rhythm off."

"Gee," interjects Rochelle. "It didn't seem to affect anyone else on your team."

What would be the best way to get Darren to take responsibility for his own shortcomings?

TEACHING YOUR CHILDREN HOW TO COPE WITH FAILURE

The most accomplished athletes do two things: 1) they take more risks — and consequently have more failures than other people, and 2) they use their failures as a way to motivate themselves and learn where they need to improve. Most poor performances are caused not by outside factors like officiating or trash talk by opponents, but by an athlete's own preoccupation with failing or messing up. Knowing that, how can you teach your children to view risk taking, mistakes, and setbacks in a more positive light?

Steps in Learning from Mistakes:

• Encourage your children to compete against themselves, not against others. Your encouragement will help them relax and perform better.

• Don't use guilt or threats to motivate your child to perform better. When you say, "You shouldn't take so many shots," or "If you don't do better, we won't be footing the bill for the lessons," you imply that failure is not acceptable to you.

• Encourage risk taking by challenging your children to try performing skills they have not yet perfected. A challenge implies that you think your children can succeed.

• Project a positive attitude about your own failures and setbacks.

• Encourage your children to ask, "What did I learn from this?" when they experience failures and setbacks.

EXERCISE

As a family (and without making fun of each other), share some of your most embarrassing sports situations or your most monumental goof-ups (sports or otherwise). Review each incident, then decide what important lesson you learned (or should have learned) from the mistake.

Discussion:

You can begin the above exercise by relating your most embarrassing sports moment. Share how you handled it and how you felt about the way you handled it ("I wish I had just laughed it off, instead of getting so upset about it").

SELF-ASSESSMENT

As a child, how did you typically respond when you made mistakes or had setbacks while playing sports? How did the way your parents, coaches, and peers reacted to your mistakes and setbacks affect you?

How did you want your parents to respond when you experienced setbacks as a child? How do you think your children want you to respond when they experience frustrations in sports?

When you experience a setback in life, do you talk about it with your family? Do you ever ask for your children's advice on how you should deal with frustrating situations?

HOW TO TEACH YOUR CHILDREN TIME-MANAGEMENT SKILLS

"Patrick, I'm worried about Rochelle," Alecia says one night. "It seems like she's hardly ever home anymore — she's either at practice, play rehearsal, or going out with that new boy she likes. And then the choir director from church called today; apparently Rochelle agreed to sing in the Easter program, too."

Patrick shrugs. "Well, you wanted her to get involved in things besides just sports."

"I know, but I think she's taken on more than she can effectively handle. When she does have free time, she just retreats to her room and 'vegges out,' as she calls it. She's not putting as much effort into her schoolwork as she used to, and I'm afraid her grades will suffer."

What can Alecia and Patrick do to help Rochelle effectively manage all the demands on her time?

HELPING YOUR CHILDREN MANAGE TIME EFFECTIVELY

Time-management skills are necessary for your children to successfully balance demands from their sports, school, and social activities. Successful student-athletes find that the only way to achieve all of their goals is to manage their time well. But just buying your children day planners will not teach them how to manage their time. What else can you do?

- Discuss time-management issues with your children to determine what the actual problem is. Maybe they do manage their time well but don't have enough time left for studying or some other important activity.
- Work with your child to identify options for freeing up time.
- Ask them to consider which of the activities they feel are most and least important to them. Encourage them to revisit the goals they have set for themselves to determine which of the activities they would feel most comfortable cutting back on.
- Offer to help them figure out ways to achieve their goals. Ultimately, they have to learn to do it themselves, but let them know you are there to support them as they try to make such changes as not procrastinating, learning to say "no" to extra activities, etc.

EXERCISE

Suggest that your children keep "time journals." These are logs of their activities for one week, where they record how much time they spend each day on each activity. At the end of the week, they should examine the time journals to see where they are spending the most time. Is it on priority items and goals?

Discussion:

Invite your children to evaluate their journals on the basis of the goals they have set for themselves. Try to ask questions that will help them establish priorities. Remember, a question such as "Which of these two activities do you consider most important?" will get better results than "What will your coach think if she learns that you are spending all that time at Starbucks each evening?"

SELF-ASSESSMENT

• How successful are you as a manager of your own time? Would it be helpful for you to join with your children in keeping and evaluating a time journal?

• How high do you think sports should be on your children's priority lists? Are you consciously or unconsciously nudging sports either up or down their lists?

• How effective do you feel you are in sharing your values with your children while communicating to them that they have to be the ones to decide what their own priorities are?

• Do you encourage your children to seek out information on their own that will help them accurately assess the consequences of how they choose to use their time? Or do you feel that it is your responsibility to point out those consequences to them?

23

HOW TO HELP YOUR CHILDREN MAKE SENSIBLE DECISIONS ABOUT TOBACCO, ALCOHOL AND DRUG USE

One look at Patrick's face lets Darren know that his dad is really upset. "Darren," Patrick says, "I understand that the police picked up several of your teammates after the game Saturday night. Apparently, they had been drinking quite heavily. These are the same friends that you told me you were going to be with that night. Were you?"

Darren looks guilty. "Yeah, I was with them for a while, but don't worry, Dad. I left before they got really plastered."

This doesn't seem to appease Patrick. "You know, Darren," he lectures, "Your mother and I always thought that because you and Rochelle are so into sports, you would know better than to abuse your bodies with drugs or alcohol. Now I'm not so sure."

"Come on, Dad," Darren whines. "It's not like the guys are a bunch of alcoholics or something!"

How should Patrick and Alecia help their children understand the consequences of tobacco, alcohol, and drug use? How can they help their children be comfortable in resisting pressure from peers?

HELPING YOUR CHILDREN RESIST PEER PRESSURE

Why is it easy for some athletes to avoid using tobacco, drugs, or alcohol when all their friends are? These kids usually care more about doing what is best for them in terms of staying healthy and in shape to compete than they do about whether resisting will hurt their images in the eyes of their peers. Kids who don't have a high regard for themselves are the ones who are dependent on others' approval to the degree that they do what others want them to do, rather than what they know is best for themselves. If you want your children to make smart choices about tobacco, drugs, and alcohol, you need to help them to become confident in their own judgment and aware of the power of peer pressure.

Tools for Resisting Peer Pressure

- Help your children understand who is calling the shots when they need to make a decision about tobacco, alcohol, or drugs. Is it a confident inner self who understands the risks involved in abusing one's body, or is it an inner self responding to peer pressure because they do not trust their own judgment?

- Help your children realize the criteria they are using to make a decision, e.g., pleasing others, popularity, etc.

- Teach your children that in a true friendship, people can say "no" without fear of being rejected.

- Recognize that your children have seen images of famous athletes promoting alcohol, chewing tobacco, and so on. Talk with your children about the mixed messages they are receiving and the real impacts such use can have on their performances in and outside the competitive arena.

EXERCISE

Have your child make up assertive responses to the following:

- A friend says, "Come on, one drink won't hurt!"

- A teammate picks you up for a party and has a six-pack in the car.

- Your date takes you to a party (in another town) where kids are drinking and using drugs.

Discussion:

Discuss with your children what it would take for them to feel comfortable in saying no if someone offered them a drink, a cigarette, or some drugs.

Discuss some of the consequences of saying no or saying yes— for example, saying no or yes to riding with someone who has a six-pack in the car. Ask how you can help them feel strong enough to resist peer pressure. Ask your children what they feel being a good friend means. Does it mean sharing the same attitudes about tobacco, alcohol, and drugs? How would they feel if a friendship ended over their refusal to do drugs or drink alcohol?

SELF-ASSESSMENT

- What role have tobacco, alcohol, and drugs played in your life?

- What is it about your personality and your upbringing that makes it easy for you to take a responsible or irresponsible position toward these substances? How can reviewing your own personal history give you some clues as to how to proceed with your own children?

- How much do you know about substance abuse?

- What kind of a role model do you present to your children in relation to substance use? How would you say your attitudes and behaviors are impacting your children?

- What would you change (if anything) to become an ideal role model for your children in relation to tobacco, alcohol, and drug use?

- How much influence did peer pressure have on you as a child? Do you feel confident in your ability to help your children in their efforts to resist peer pressure? In what areas might you need to learn more to help your children?

HOW TO HELP YOUR CHILDREN AVOID EATING DISORDERS

Patrick looks at Rochelle, who is pushing her food around on her plate.

"What's the matter, Rochelle? You've hardly been eating the past few days. Don't you feel well?"

"I feel fine," Rochelle replies. "I'm just getting too fat is all."

"Says who?" Patrick responds.

"The coach. She's been weighing us in twice a week and measuring our body fat. She says my body fat count is too high. Can you spell C-O-W?"

"Don't be silly, Rochelle," says Alecia, joining the conversation. "You look fine. And if you don't start eating sensibly, you're not going to have any energy. Did your coach mention THAT?"

"Darren, you tell them!" Rochelle says, dragging her brother into the debate. "I have a rear end the size of Texas! You always say so!" Darren tries to look innocent. "Oh, none of you understand!" Rochelle cries, stomping out of the room. "I wish you'd all just leave me alone!"

Should Patrick and Alecia be concerned about Rochelle's eating pattern? How should they deal with this situation?

RECOGNIZING SIGNS OF EATING DISORDERS

It can be difficult for parents to recognize or admit to signs of eating disorders in their children. However, increasing numbers of girls and boys are falling victim to these diseases. Because of the extra emphasis that is placed on weight and body image in the world of sports (in addition to the American cultural standard of thinness), athletes can be especially susceptible to eating disorders. What can you do to help your child avoid eating disorders?

- Be observant. Signs of eating disorders include eating tiny portions or refusing to eat; rapid weight loss without any other cause; intense fear of being fat; excessive exercise; eating in secret; disappearing after eating, often going to the bathroom; great fluctuations in weight; loss of menstrual cycle in girls; dependency on laxatives, diuretics, or diet pills.

- Understand that the eating disorder is only a symptom of a deeper problem. In other words, you need to help your child identify and solve that problem before you can resolve the eating disorder.

- Recognize the importance of seeking professional help, both for you and your child. Eating disorders are serious, serious illnesses that can rarely be solved without outside help. If you suspect that one of your children is developing an eating disorder, you should consult your family physician or the school counselor.

EXERCISE

As a family, prepare a poster using newspaper and magazine clippings that depict "ideal" body images. Next, do some reading or talk to a teacher to determine the average sizes of men and women in the U.S. List these figures on the poster. How do the pictures compare with reality?

Discussion:

Ask family members where they think these "ideal" body images come from. Discuss how these images influence their views of their bodies. Consider how people feel who do not conform to this ideal. Discuss ways that young people can limit the impact of these images on their ways of thinking about themselves.

SELF-ASSESSMENT

• How important is body image to you? What subtle messages might you be communicating to your children about body image?

• Do you talk about your own weight problems with your children? Do you comment on other people's weight or size to your children? Might your comments place extra importance on body size?

• Do you or your children subscribe to glamour or fitness magazines? If so, do you make an effort to use these magazines to raise your children's consciousness about images portrayed by the media?

• Do you often suggest to your children that they eat more or less than they do? What are you communicating with these suggestions?

HOW TO HELP YOUR CHILDREN CHOOSE GOOD ROLE MODELS

"You know, Dad," Darren says as Patrick is driving him to school one morning, "I really admire the coach. He's always ready to defend us if he thinks the refs aren't making the right calls. He doesn't take any crap from anybody!"

"I noticed he got all over the refs the other night when they blew that call against J.R."

"That's what I mean! We can always count on the coach to support us, even if it means he gets thrown out of a game. If I ever coach, I hope I can be as good as he is."

Patrick doesn't know how to respond to these remarks. On the one hand, he wants his son to be loyal to the coach. However, Patrick doesn't think the way the coach always argues with the refs shows respect for the job the officials do. And, if the truth be told, he's a little jealous of Darren's intense admiration for the man.

What options does Patrick have in how he responds to Darren's comments about the coach? What are the costs and benefits of each of these options?

CHOOSING GOOD SPORTS ROLE MODELS

The primary way children learn their attitudes, values, skills, and standards of behavior is by watching and imitating other people. A role model is an individual whose actions a person decides are worthy of imitation. But how a parent defines "worthy" and their children define "worthy" aren't always the same. Here are some steps you can take to help your children learn how to select good role models:

- Start by learning who your children's role models are. Ask them to explain how they selected their role models. What characteristics did they consider in selecting the sports personalities they most admire and want to be like?

- Suggest additional factors they might consider in choosing a role model. The list could include:

    - Competency (someone who is successful in a certain area);

    - Perceived similarity (children are more likely to imitate individuals who share similar interests);

    - Credibility (a person's actions should be consistent with the behaviors they promote — for example, an athlete who projects a "family" image shouldn't be arrested for hitting someone);

    - Enthusiasm (someone who promotes a "can-do" attitude);

    - Respect (someone who respects and is respected by others);

    - Compassion (someone who exhibits warmth and caring toward others).

- Talk to your children about a sports figure whom you admire and explain how that person exhibits these qualities.

EXERCISE

Have a family contest to select a sports role model. Each member of the family should submit his or her favorite candidate and give reasons to support that candidate (you can use the criteria listed above as suggested factors to consider in making their selections). After hearing from everyone, family members can then select the role models who seem to embody the greatest number of desired characteristics.

Discussion:

A lively debate among family members "campaigning" for different candidates as role models can provoke careful consideration of the factors that go into choosing an ideal sports figure. It is important to have each person clearly elaborate how he or she has made his or her choice and to point out (and celebrate) the common values that your family holds.

SELF-ASSESSMENT

• Who were your sports heroes as a child? Who are your current heroes? How do they compare with each other? What has happened to influence your choices over the years?

• In what ways do you think you are influencing your children's choices of sports role models? How do you think you can most effectively influence your children's choices of role models?

• What kind of a sports role model are you, as a player, a spectator, and a parent? What things do you do (or fail to do) to embody the values you want to promote with your children? In what areas do you need to improve to be a better role model?

HOW TO MAKE EVERYONE A WINNER

Patrick and Alecia are excited. Rochelle's team is about to play its biggest game of the season. Rochelle and her teammates play the best game ever — unfortunately, they lose by a narrow margin. As the girls dejectedly trudge off the field, Alecia notices that some of them don't even bother shaking hands with their opponents. She can also see tears rolling down many of their cheeks, which doesn't surprise her very much. What does surprise her, however, are the tears she sees on the faces of some of the parents, and even the coach!

"Did I miss something?" she asks Patrick. "I know they lost, but they played incredibly well. Didn't anyone notice that part of it?"

What can Alecia and Patrick do to help Rochelle and her teammates see that there are other ways of "winning" besides scoring the most points?

INSTILLING A "WIN-WIN" OUTLOOK

From competitive sports to political elections, our society has long been based on the win-lose premise. Getting children (and parents) to think in terms of win-win can be challenging, but rewarding. Even though the reality in sports is that only one team ends up with the most points on the scoreboard, parents can still do things to instill a win-win spirit in their children. One of the most important concepts to consider is that no individual athlete or team can ultimately control the outcome of a contest. Focusing on striving for the best performance is all an individual can really control. By talking to your children about this fact regularly, you can make a real difference in their abilities to develop a win-win outlook.

Encouraging a Win-Win Outlook:

- Encourage your children to look for points of personal improvement. Since your children can only control how they themselves perform, they are ultimately competing with themselves each time they take the field. They can consider themselves winners whenever they master a skill or achieve a personal goal.

- Encourage your children to help others do their best. Help them understand the rewards that come from helping their teammates achieve their own personal sports dreams or from challenging their opponents to do their best by pushing them to their limits.

- Be sure you make the effort to reward your children when you see them doing things to spur themselves, their teammates, or their opponents to play better.

- Avoid asking questions like "Who won?" Instead, ask your children what things they think they are improving on.

- When you and your children see or read about a professional, college, or other team losing when everyone thought they would win, use it as an opportunity to talk about how little control anyone has over the outcome of a contest.

EXERCISE

Create a "win-win" score card that can be used to record a variety of things that are part of sports competition (e.g., the beauty of the performances, the enthusiasm the athletes show, the teamwork displayed, the way the coach uses substitutes, etc.). Assign a point value (such as 1-5, with 1 being "poor" and 5 being "excellent") that can be used to rate each of these items. Schedule a time when your family can all watch (either on television or in person) a sports competition. Have each family member "score" the competition using the "win-win" score cards. Compare cards and discuss any differences in scoring. Invite your children to use the score cards to judge their own practices and competitions. (This is an exercise that you will probably have to do several times to make changes in how your family habitually views sports.)

Discussion:

After completing the above exercise for the first time, did anyone think of additional items that should be added to the win-win score card (such as the quality of the refreshments or the enthusiasm of the fans)? Did using the win-win card help you notice these little things more than you normally would? How did using the win-win card change how family members viewed the over-all competition? Was it more, less, or equally enjoyable? Is this activity some-thing family members would like to do more often?

SELF-ASSESSMENT

What childhood experiences can you think of that have contributed to your attitudes toward athletic competition? How ingrained are these attitudes? Can you change them if you need to?

Are you still using a win-lose outlook in your sports life? How big a gap is there between where you are and where you may want to go?

What have been the consequences for you of employing a win-lose ap-proach to sports? What have been the consequences to your children?

What do you think will be the barriers for you and your family to learning a win-win approach to sports? Do you think your family would agree with this list?

HOW TO ACCENTUATE THE POSITIVE

Darren's team has lost four in a row. Patrick is reading about the previous day's loss. When Darren walks in and sees the headline, he immediately growls, "That's a bunch of @#$%!"

"Darren, watch your language!" Alecia warns.

"Oh, lighten up, Mom," Darren responds. "It's not your starting position on the line."

"Don't worry, Darren," Patrick interjects. "You guys would've had that game if the refs hadn't been so obviously in favor of the home team."

Alecia frowns. "Patrick, now you're starting to sound like some of the other parents."

Patrick smiles sheepishly. "You're right. I guess all this negativity is contagious."

What can Alecia and Patrick do to foster a more positive attitude and make their experiences with this team more enjoyable and productive?

INSPIRING POSITIVE THINKING IN
YOUR ATHLETIC CHILDREN

As a sports parent, you've probably seen your young athletes fall victim to at least one of the following negative thought patterns:

Catastrophizing: Predicting the worst outcome. "If we lose the game, I'll lose my starting position."

Overgeneralizing: Assuming something will always happen. "We're gonna lose. We always lose."

Exaggerating: Making negative things more important than they are. "We lost the championship! My whole life is ruined."

Black and White Thinking: Thinking in extremes. "If I can't be a starter, then I'm gonna quit!"

Successful sports parents know that when they or their children give in to negative thinking, it impacts their performances (as parents or athletes) and makes sports less enjoyable and rewarding for themselves and those around them. So how can you and your children recognize negative thoughts and replace them with good ones?

1. When you or your children feel upset, identify the thoughts that are troubling you.

2. For each troubling thought, think of a different way of looking at it (e.g., "That was the worst game of my life." "Actually, I've played worse before, and I'm still on the team.")

3. Replace the negative thought with a positive one. ("I'll practice hard and my next game will be better.")

EXERCISE

To raise your family's consciousness about the toxic nature of negative thoughts, have your family make a list of as many negative thoughts as you can think of that go through: 1) an athlete's head, and 2) a parent's head, during a practice or competition. List these thoughts on two separate sheets of paper posted on the wall. For each negative thought listed, come up with a positive "replacement" thought.

Discussion:

Looking at the list of negative thoughts that athletes sometimes have, discuss what effect putting these thoughts into words might have on the athlete's teammates, coach, parents, or other parents and spectators. Discuss what effect putting the parents' negative thoughts into words might have on their children, the coach, their partners, or other parents and spectators.

SELF-ASSESSMENT

- When things go wrong in your life, do you tend to dwell on the negative or try to put a positive spin on it? Would you say that, overall, you model a positive or a negative attitude for your children?

- When you reflect on the thoughts you have as you watch your children's sports events, would you say they are generally positive or negative?

- What factors do you feel have caused you to develop your positive or negative outlook on sports? How have your own sports experiences influenced how you look at your children's sports experiences?

- How much have you invested (money, time, etc.) in your children's sports lives? Do you ever (consciously or unconsciously) encourage your children to do well in sports "because we've spent all this money on lessons"?

HOW TO BE SENSITIVE TO SIBLING RIVALRY

"Hey, Mom, look! Here's another story about me in the paper!" Darren grabs the sports section out of his sister's hands and waves it over his head.

"Hey, you dweeb! Give that back! I was reading it!" Rochelle tries to yank the paper out of her brother's hands.

"Reading about your famous brother who's the first athlete in the state to be selected to attend the best sports academy in the country?" Darren brags.

Rochelle groans. "Give me a break. Just because everyone else in the family is falling all over you right now doesn't mean I am. Now give me the paper so I can read about something interesting — like how everyone else is doing."

How should the Hawkins family deal with the challenges of having more attention given to one child than the other?

DISTRIBUTING YOUR ATTENTION

When it comes to sibling rivalry, many parents make the mistake of reacting to it <u>after</u> it happens instead of establishing a "game plan" to deal with it <u>before</u> it happens. Positive sports parents recognize that sports are a breeding ground for sibling rivalry. You need to prepare yourself ahead of time to identify those specific situations that provoke rivalry in your children. Then you and your children can develop strategies for coping with these situations. The most effective strategy, naturally, is to listen to your children:

- Instead of telling your children how they're supposed to feel ("You should be proud of your brother's score!"), ask them to tell you how they really feel. Encourage them tell you the truth.

- Take (or make) time to talk with each child separately about their sports experiences.

- Ask for your children's input on solving any sibling rivalry problems that might arise. Ask questions like: What upsets you most about your brother/ sister's sports involvement? Do you think Mom and Dad are handling things fairly, or do you think we take sides?

- Ask your child to consider what it would be like to have one of the greatest sports heroes in history as a brother or sister (pick someone whom your child respects if possible). Then ask if the attention generated publicly by that hero means that the sibling is any less valuable or important. Emphasize the importance of striving to be the best person possible with whatever talents have been bestowed upon you.

EXERCISE

As a way of getting your children to take some of the responsibility for reducing the impact of sibling rivalry, ask them to suggest some solutions to the problem of fairness they feel will benefit the whole family. Work with them to develop a set of guidelines that you, as parents, can follow to avoid the appearance of favoring one child over another. (Avoid getting defensive at their suggestions!) Follow that task by asking your children to create a list of guidelines they can follow that will help them be more supportive of each other.

Discussion:

Explain to your children that you don't expect them to be perfect — it's perfectly natural to feel a little jealous or envious when the spotlight is turned on someone else. Remind them, however, that one of your goals as a family should be to always be supportive of each other. Discuss the possibility of coming up with a "code word" that family members could use to signal when one of them is feeling the need for extra attention. This could help children avoid the need to pout, fuss, or otherwise act out when they are feeling over-looked.

SELF-ASSESSMENT

• When you were growing up, did you experience any sibling rivalry when it came to sports? How did your parents handle it? What impact did it have on your enthusiasm for sports? What impact did it have on your siblings and your relationship with them?

• How do your childhood experiences with sibling rivalry affect how you try to parent your children? For example, if you always felt that your parents showed more attention to a more athletic brother or sister, do you find yourself giving more time and attention to your non-athletic children at the expense of your athletic child?

• How effective are you at reducing the negative impact of sibling rivalry on your family? What actions have you taken recently that demonstrate you have been successful in fairly distributing your attention to your children? What things have you said or done that you wish you hadn't? What could you have done to avoid these mistakes?

29

HOW TO HELP YOUR CHILDREN DEAL WITH A CONTROLLING COACH

Alecia is aware that Rochelle has been stewing for weeks about which classes she should take during the upcoming school year. That's why she's surprised when Rochelle comes home one day, tosses her class schedule on the counter, and says, "Whew! I'm glad that's done!"

"You decided what classes you want?" Alecia asks.

"It was easy!" Rochelle exclaims. "I talked with my coach, and she told me exactly what to take. She said I should have gone to her at the beginning and saved myself a lot of trouble."

Alecia looks over the list of classes. "Rochelle," she says. "There's only one advanced-placement class on this list. You qualified for three of them."

"Yeah, but coach says that many AP classes will take up too much time. She said I'm better off putting my efforts into a sports scholarship. And you know what else she said? She said forget about Stanford—UCLA would be the better school for me!"

Alecia frowns. "Don't you think that's a decision for you to make—not your coach?"

How should the Hawkins family deal with situations in which they feel coaches are exerting too much control over their children?

ENCOURAGING YOUR CHILDREN TO TAKE CHARGE OF THEIR OWN SPORTS LIVES

There are many reasons to be concerned about coaches who exert too much control over your children's lives (some of which are discussed in other areas of this book). High on the list is the fact that the more control athletes give up to other people, the less able they are to develop independence, take charge of their sports careers, and become their own people. Professional sports provide many examples of athletes who seem lost once their playing days end. You can help your children avoid being suffocated by a controlling coach by encouraging them to develop the kind of independence that will allow them to chart the courses of their own sports experiences.

What Sports-Related Tasks Can You Encourage Your Children to Be Responsible For?

- Waking themselves up for early morning practice
- Washing their uniforms
- Informing you of and making arrangements for transportation to practices
- Completing independent weight-training and running assignments
- Putting in extra practice time prescribed by the coach
- Paying for athletic shoes and/or other expenses associated with their sports program
- Participating in team fundraisers
- Thinking about what they can do to make sports participation now pay the biggest possible dividends in their lives later

EXERCISE

Before each sports season begins, conduct a family meeting where you:

- Review the coaches' requirements with your children.

• Make a list of

   - The various tasks that need to be done (get physicals, pur-
   chase uniforms, etc.) prior to your children's participation in
   their sports programs;

   - The tasks that need to be done once the sports programs
   begin (arrange a driving schedule, practice skills, wash uniforms, etc.).

• Note who is currently responsible for making sure the above tasks
are performed.

• Agree upon who should be performing the tasks.

• Have your children sign off on the tasks they have agreed to perform.

Discussion:

Since parents of young athletes begin their children's athletic careers by
performing nearly all of the above "sports chores," it is sometimes difficult for
children to assume responsibility for these tasks as they get older. Discuss
with your children the importance of learning responsibility (to make it more
appealing to them, you might want to bring up the fact that increased responsibility often brings increased privilege). You will find that although they may
complain about it, most children enjoy the satisfaction that comes with successfully carrying out a responsibility. Also discuss the consequences of not
fulfilling a responsibility. (For example, children who are consistently late getting in the car to go to practice might be informed that for every minute they are
late, they will have to sit in the car before getting out to join their teammates at
practice. Five minutes of sitting in the parking lot while their coach and teammates impatiently wait for them will quickly cure the tardiness issue!)

SELF-ASSESSMENT

- When you were a child, who assumed responsibility for your sports chores? Were you well-prepared to take responsibility for yourself, or did you depend too much on others?

- How much do you currently depend on your partner to perform your sports chores for you or for your children?

- What methods do you use to encourage your children to take responsibility for their sports chores? Do you tend to nag or lecture them? Do you give in and do things yourself? How effective do you feel your methods are?

- Do you have the patience to stand by while your children struggle to learn how to take responsibility for their lives in sports? Do you and your partner support each other in your efforts to teach responsibility, even if it means allowing your children to fail to fulfill their obligations?

30

HOW TO HELP YOUR CHILDREN DEAL
WITH AN ABUSIVE COACH

"Rochelle!" Darren calls. "Telephone!" Rochelle runs to answer the phone.

"Please tell me it's not another boy," Patrick says, rolling his eyes in exasperation. "She's already had four phone calls tonight, and each one of them has been from a boy."

"Well, it's not exactly a boy," Darren answers. "It's the assistant coach from her team."

"Again? Didn't he just call a couple of nights ago?"

Alecia joins in the conversation. "Rochelle said he likes to discuss game strategies with her, since she's the team captain."

"We've never had a coach do that before," Patrick comments. "Don't you think it's odd?"

"At least Rochelle's coach is nice to her," Darren says. "All my coach does is scream at us guys and call us 'lard butt' and 'lame brain.'"

What should Alecia and Patrick do to recognize and prevent abusive coaching?

PREVENTING ABUSE OF ATHLETES

The two most common reasons kids give for quitting sports are: 1) the sport is no longer fun, and 2) they feel abused by their coaches. What can you do to help ensure that your children do not become victimized, either sexually, physically, or psychologically, by a trusted coach? While the following tips apply mainly to the area of sexual abuse, many apply equally well to physical and verbal abuse.

- Get to know your child's coach. Ask about his or her qualifications; discuss training rules and standards of behavior.

- Attend practices and games to watch the coach in action. Observe how the coach interacts with the children; observe how other parents and kids respond to the coach's style and/or behavior.

- Talk to your children about the coach, and listen to how they and their teammates talk about the coach.

- Help your children recognize when a coach's behavior is inappropriate (signs include using demeaning language; hitting or pushing athletes; spending time alone with an athlete; and touching the athlete inappropriately when demonstrating sports skills).

- Trust your instincts. If you're feeling uncomfortable about the coach, try to identify why. Discuss your feelings with someone who can give you objective feedback on whether you're on target or over-reacting.

- Talk to program administrators about whether coaches have undergone criminal background checks prior to being hired.

EXERCISE

Role play with your children what they would do in one of the following situations: 1) While demonstrating a sports skill, the coach touches the athlete in a way that makes him or her feel uncomfortable, but is not blatant sexual touching; 2) While alone with the athlete, the coach starts talking about some of his or her family (or marital) problems and mentions how close he or she feels to the athlete; 3) After the athlete makes a bad play, the coach grabs him or her by the arm and physically throws them onto a chair.

Discussion:

This exercise can be an uncomfortable one for many children, because of the nature of the issue. You need to communicate to your children that you have confidence in their abilities to make good judgments, but that if they are caught by surprise, they need to be prepared to make wise choices. Reassure your children that you trust their coaches and do not expect anything bad to happen, but that you want them to be prepared in case such an incident should ever occur.

SELF-ASSESSMENT:

• How good are you at communicating with your children about sensitive subjects? Do you feel that they would open up to you if they felt uncomfortable about a coach's actions?

• Do you build up trust with your children by listening to them when they want to talk to you about their concerns, even if you don't feel it's anything "important"?

• Have you been either physically, psychologically, or sexually abused by a coach? How have your past experiences with coaches influenced how you view the issue of abuse?

31

HOW TO CONSULT YOUR FAMILY BEFORE COACHING YOUR CHILDREN'S TEAMS

"Guess what, Alecia?" Patrick says as he arrives home from work. "I got a call today asking me if I'd be interested in coaching Darren's club team. What do you think?"

"What do you think?" Alecia counters. "You're certainly qualified."

"Yeah, that's not the problem," Patrick says. "I guess I'm concerned about how Darren and I would get along if I were his coach. I think we have a pretty good relationship now, but so did Bruce Armstrong and his son — until they asked Bruce to coach. Remember what happened? They almost ended up in family counseling!"

What factors should Patrick consider in making his decision about whether to coach his son's team?

MAKING DECISIONS AS A FAMILY

To coach or not to coach? Since the answer to that question will ultimately affect everyone in the family, positive sports parents recognize the importance of involving the entire family in the decision. When making decisions as a family, you should ask:

- What is the problem, or question, to be decided? Everyone should be free to express their views without judgment. For example, a child should be free to say, "Dad wants to screw up my life by coaching my team!"

- What are the key issues involved? Mom's issue might be concern over how much time coaching will involve. Dad's issue might be a desire to recreate some of his childhood sports experiences. Junior's issue could be a fear that the other kids will tease him for being the "coach's pet."

• What solution is acceptable to everyone? Maybe Dad could coach a different team — that way he could experience the fun of coaching without putting his child in a potentially uncomfortable situation.

EXERCISE

Hold a family meeting to discuss the issue of having you or your partner coach one of your children's sports teams. Begin by making a list of the characteristics of an ideal coach. Then, make a list of characteristics of an ideal sports parent. Compare the two lists. Ask family members to identify items on the lists that could create problems for a parent who is trying to do both jobs.

Discussion:

Since parents who choose to coach their children's teams aren't the only ones affected by the decision, ask your children what kinds of problems they might face in trying to be a good team member and a good family member. Discuss what would make it possible for both the parent/coach and the child/athlete to work together effectively. Discuss how the decision to take on a coaching assignment could affect the other members of the family as well.

SELF-ASSESSMENT

• Were you ever coached by one of your parents? If you were, what kind of experience was it for you? If you weren't, how successful of an experience do you think it would have been?

• What kind of emotional history do you have with your children? Is there any "old baggage" that a player/coach relationship might bring up?

• What are your reasons for wanting to coach your children?

• How strong are your relationships with the children you would not be coaching? How do you think they will respond to the attention you are giving their sibling? Do you have a game plan in place for dealing with sibling rivalry in this area?

HOW TO CONSIDER THE PROS AND CONS OF TEACHING SPORTS SKILLS TO YOUR CHILDREN

Rochelle's position on her team is being threatened because she has not developed some of the basic fundamentals. Patrick wants to help Rochelle learn these skills. He feels that he has the expertise to help her be a starter on a team that is sure to be a contender for a regional title.

However, Alecia is concerned that if Patrick tries to teach Rochelle the skills, it will not only sour their father/daughter relationship, but get Patrick in trouble with Rochelle's coach as well.

"Remember, dear," Alecia comments to her husband, "when Rochelle wanted me to teach her how to sew, I told her she'd just have to learn it in Home Ec. Sometimes it's just a lot easier for kids to learn things from someone they're not close to."

Under what circumstances, if any, should a parent undertake the task of teaching their children sports skills? If parents do decide to teach their children, what approach is most effective?

GIVING CONSTRUCTIVE FEEDBACK

Kids grow up getting a lot of feedback from their parents about virtually every aspect of their lives. This is why it can be hard for them to learn a sports skill from their parents—they automatically put up the "criticism barrier" and tune out or get defensive about what's being said. If you decide to teach your children how to perform a sports skill, you cannot avoid having to correct them. You can, however, improve your chances of getting your children to listen and learn from you by improving your feedback skills.

Dos and Don'ts of Constructive Sports Feedback

- DON'T turn your feedback into a power struggle about who's right.
- DO be specific. ("Hold your elbow in on your shot.")
- DON'T generalize. ("You always do it the wrong way!")
- DO use a calm and controlled voice. Kids can't perform well when someone's angry at them.
- DON'T use name calling, labeling, or sarcastic comments. ("You're such a klutz sometimes!")
- DO watch for signs that your child needs a break. A lack of progress or repeated mistakes from an apparent lack of concentration may be signs that your child wants or needs to stop practicing and do something else.
- DON'T keep repeating yourself. If your feedback isn't being understood, either rephrase what you're saying or ask your child to tell you what he or she thinks you're saying.
- DO get the consent of your child's coach to work with your child. Review with the coach the techniques he or she prefers to have you teach.
- DON'T undermine the coach's efforts at teaching your child. When you disagree with the coach about a technique or style issue, talk to the coach about your view and come to agreement on what should be done to avoid putting your child in a difficult, confusing situation.
- DO brush up on your own knowledge and technique. Some time may have passed since you were playing or coaching yourself. Do some reading and/ or talk to the coach to make sure you are providing your child with the best instruction possible.

EXERCISE

Let your children experience the challenge of being a teacher. Have each one teach you something that you don't know (like a sports skill or some other skill) while trying to use the principles of constructive feedback.

Discussion:

With your children, discuss how the above exercise felt and what each of you learned from the experience. For example, were your children satisfied with their teaching efforts? What did they think they did well? What do they wish they had done better? Was any part of the exercise frustrating for them? For you? Would they want you to teach them exactly the way they taught you? Why or why not?

SELF-ASSESSMENT

• Do you have sufficient sports skill and knowledge to be able to teach your children effectively? Do you have a solid understanding of sports fundamentals?

• Do you have the patience to teach your own children, or would someone else among your family or friends be better suited to the task?

• Would teaching your children sports skills improve, harm, or make no difference to your relationship with them?

• Can you accept honest feedback from your children regarding the effectiveness of your teaching? Are you willing to ask them for suggestions on how you can improve your teaching skills?

HOW TO CREATE AN ENVIRONMENT WHERE GOOD SPORTSMANSHIP PREVAILS

Patrick and Alecia are sitting in the stands watching the long-anticipated game between Darren's basketball team and their arch-rivals. Several rows away, Rochelle and her friends are cheering boisterously. At one point, when an opposing player is knocked to the floor and is slow to get up, Rochelle and her friends begin yelling comments like, "What a baby!" "Somebody call his mommy!"

Disturbed, Alecia turns to Patrick, "Did you hear what your daughter –" she begins, but is interrupted by Patrick jumping to his feet to 'boo' loudly when the referee calls a technical on one of Darren's teammates.

What can the Hawkinses do to encourage an atmosphere of good sports-manship at their children's athletic events?

RAISING GOOD SPORTS

Sportsmanship is just another word for consideration. When you teach your children to play fair and encourage their teammates and other players, you are teaching them to consider the welfare of other human beings. Most children develop consideration without too much difficulty, but this characteristic needs to be nurtured or it can wither away. To point your children in the right direction:

• Be an example. Do you "boo" when the referee makes a bad call? Do you downplay the skills of others to make your child feel better? Or do your children see you walking over to the opposing fans after a game to congratulate them on their athletes? You can preach sportsmanship until you are blue in the face, but if you don't model it, your kids won't learn it.

• Encourage empathy. Help your children put themselves in another's place by asking them how they would feel if they were in the same situation — for example, if they were the ones who had just lost a close game because of a poor call by a referee.

• Encourage social responsibility. Some school and club teams routinely make service projects part of their season. Involving children in charitable programs helps them learn consideration for others.

EXERCISE

Develop a family code of conduct to serve as a guide for how your family would like to behave at athletic events. Have each member of the family list items that he or she thinks should be included in the set of guidelines. Determine whether everyone is prepared to live by the code. Then develop a family "sportsmanship" motto. Think of as many words as you can that relate to the ideas of sportsmanship that you have included in your code of conduct. Choose one or two words to create that motto that reflects your family's feelings about sportsmanship. For example: "Fair and square," or "Kindness first!"

Discussion:

Ask your family if they feel creating a code and a motto will be enough to develop an enduring commitment to sportsmanship. Discuss with your family positive ways that you can continually remind and encourage one another to be good sports (for example, you could create a "Good Sport of the Week" award to be handed out at your weekly family meeting).

SELF-ASSESSMENT

• What kind of sportsmanship did you exhibit as a young athlete? Did your sportsmanship improve or deteriorate as you got older?

• How do you behave at your children's competitions? Do you preach sportsmanship to your children without exhibiting it yourself?

• Do you have the ability to be inspired by and show respect for all the participants at your children's sporting events?

• On a scale of 1 to 10, with 10 being an excellent sport, where would you rate yourself as a sports parent? As a competitor? As a spectator of professional sports competitions? Are there differences in any of these scores? Should there be?

34

HOW TO HELP MAKE SPORTS
FUN, FESTIVE, AND FRIENDLY

While driving home from one of Darren's games, Alecia says to Patrick, "Is it just me, or is this season less fun than last season was?"

"What do you mean?" Patrick asks.

"I don't know. There just seems to be a lot of contentiousness out there. The players don't support each other, the coach is always in somebody's face, and the parents are always complaining about the officiating. It wasn't like this last year."

"Well, last year we were a young team and we weren't expected to win. This year, we are. We've got a lot of seniors who are looking for scholarships. There's more pressure. Face it, Alecia, this is what the 'big leagues' are like — so we might as well get used to it."

"I don't agree!" Alecia responds with a touch of anger. "You know what these games remind me of now? Going to church and having one of the parishioners jump up and start shouting comments during the sermon. It breaks the spell that a church service can cast. The way people have been acting at these games has broken the spell of sports for me, Patrick."

How are negative practices in some professional and college sports affecting youth sports programs? What can Alecia do to help make sports fun again?

"SHARING THE VISION" OF A POSITIVE SPORTS CLIMATE

A positive sports climate is one that makes athletes feel comfortable enough to take risks. It is uplifting and supportive for everyone — athletes, coaches, parents, and fans. What can parents do to create this kind of climate? The most critical thing is to make a concerted effort to inspire other parents to share your dream of a fun, festive, and friendly youth sports program. You can do this by:

1. Seeking to understand what other parents want from their youth sports program;

2. Demonstrating (through your own behavior) how everyone will benefit from creating a positive sports climate;

3. Communicating your passion for creating a positive sports climate by:

   • Using vivid images and word pictures to describe your vision, along with examples everyone can relate to ("Remember when we were kids — the smell of the hotdogs, the sound of the ball hitting the mitt? Let's try to bring that feeling back for everyone!");

   • Appealing to common beliefs and values ("We're all here because we want our kids to have fun, right?");

   • Being enthusiastic ("Serve on the fund-raising committee? I'd love to!");

   • "Adopting" all the kids on your children's teams, treating them with the same support and enthusiasm you would show toward your own children; and

   • Working to build a team community or culture that allows the athletes and their families to feel special.

EXERCISE

Dr. Martin Luther King, Jr.'s "I Have a Dream" speech is a great example of communicating a shared vision. Using his speech and/or the suggestions above, draft your own speech (either alone or working with another parent or parents who share your feelings) in support of creating a more positive sports climate for your youth sports program. Share this at your next parents' meeting and/or in a letter to the editor of your local newspaper.

Discussion:

Share an early draft of your speech with your family. What is their reaction? Do they have any comments or suggestions for improvements? Do they feel it successfully captures how your family feels about sports?

SELF-ASSESSMENT

- Do you believe your children can still learn to be "tough" in a "tender" sports environment? In other words, do you believe that children can learn how to play competitively and aggressively while exhibiting care and concern for their teammates and opponents?

- Do you feel that a sports environment that plays down conflict and contentiousness is "coddling" your children?

- What role do you feel parents play in determining whether a sports event will be an uplifting one or not? As an athlete and a parent, how successful have you been at helping to create a positive sports climate?

- What experiences have you had that lead you to believe your children's sports programs can be guided by your dream of a better world of sports?

- What skills do you have or need to develop to exercise leadership in creating a positive sports climate?

35

HOW TO CREATE A CLIMATE
THAT IS FAMILY FRIENDLY

"You know, Patrick," Alecia observes as they sit in the bleachers for one of Rochelle's games, "this is the third game we've been to this season, and so far they've all been the same. Hardly any parents show up, and the ones that do don't seem to make much of an effort to talk to each other. Don't you think that says something?"

"I think it says that the parents just want to concentrate on their kids' performances without being distracted by 'chit-chat,'" Patrick replies, as he scans the field for Rochelle.

"Well, I think it says the coach hasn't done a very good job of involving the parents."

"You can't put all the blame on the coach," Patrick says. "Maybe she's had some bad experiences with parents in the past. She's probably gotten tired of parents who are either too busy to support their kids, or, at the other extreme, are over involved in their kids' sports lives. Not all parents are as perfect as we are, you know!"

Alecia laughs. "Seriously, Patrick, it seems like there's almost a trend these days to run youth sports like a business and keep the families out of it. Don't you think we should do something to make things more family friendly?"

What can Alecia and the other parents do to make sure the sports program encourages more family input and involvement?

ENCOURAGING FAMILY-FRIENDLY SPORTS PROGRAMS

Youth sports programs are bastions of tradition. Thus, it can be challenging to try to initiate changes that help a program be more family friendly. However, parents who believe strongly in the family-friendly platform must be willing to speak up and take risks for the sake of changing the business-as-usual environment. Part of that risk involves questioning those practices that fit the description "That's the way we've always done it."

Questioning the status quo:

• Be up front with the coach about your desire to encourage a family-friendly climate, and enlist his or her support for helping you achieve this objective.

• Coaches are sometimes suspicious of parent involvement in their sports programs because they've had too many experiences with self-serving parents, parents who are out to promote their children's careers, or parents who are control freaks who want to take over coaching functions. Thus, any efforts to initiate a review of program policies and practices are likely to be resisted by the coach, unless you reach an agreement on which policies should remain the exclusive province of the coach and which could be modified by the parent community to make the program more family friendly.

• For each policy or practice, ask: "How useful is this for helping the team become the best it can be?" "How useful is it for encouraging families to participate in meaningful, uplifting sports experiences?"

• Keep in mind that, while coaches and parents are both working toward a common goal of helping young people, their approaches are fundamentally different in at least one important way. As a parent, your job is to look out for the best interests of your children. Your coach's job, on the other hand, is to look out for the best interests of all the children on the team. When what is best for one child means a sacrifice for other children or for the team, coaches and parents are more likely to come into conflict. Approach this dilemma by recognizing that your children will be members of teams throughout their lives. The most successful people have been those who were able to put aside personal interests to make it possible for a team to do something greater than any individual ever could. When these kinds of conflicts arise—either through policies or situations that arise—avoid saying or doing anything until you have asked yourself whether there's a potential lesson to be learned about the value of teams and teamwork.

EXERCISE

With the coach's consent, enlist some interested parents to join you in assessing current team policies and practices to determine how they contribute to or prevent the creation of a family-friendly sports environment. In conducting the policy review:

• Talk to all the other team parents and ask them for their suggestions on what would make their families feel more included and involved in the program;

• Present your findings and suggestions to the coach or program administrator in a helpful, non-confrontational manner. Help them see the intrinsic rewards that will come to the team, to their families, and also to the coach through incorporating family-friendly policies and practices into their program.

Discussion:

Before taking your ideas to your coach, rehearse your presentation in front of another team parent. Ask if it sounds like you are challenging your coach's authority or implying that he or she is incompetent. If he or she were the coach listening to your presentation, what would his or her reaction be?

SELF-ASSESSMENT

- Do you have the courage to lead an effort to transform the team's culture from one focused primarily upon learning sports skills and winning competitions to one that extends the focus to include renewing the spirits of participants and enriching their families?

- Do you feel confident enough to take steps with the coach and other parents to make the program more family friendly? Do you have the leadership skills that will allow you to mobilize the support of your fellow parents, many of whom may very well be uninterested in rocking the boat? If you don't have the skills, would you be willing to learn them?

- Do you feel comfortable in recruiting other parents to be your allies? Can you do so in a way that is not seen as challenging the coach?

36

HOW TO INVEST IN FORMING AN INSPIRING SPORTS COMMUNITY

"Patrick! I've got a great idea!" Alecia exclaims. "How about every time one of the players on Rochelle's team gets a hit, all the dads get down and do ten push-ups? And we moms could cheer you on!"

Patrick laughs. "Al Johnson would probably have a heart attack."

"Come on," Alecia cajoles, "I'm just trying to think of ways to get everyone more 'into' the games. I've noticed that everyone — players, coaches, parents — seem to enjoy the experience more when we're all involved and supporting one another. Remember the first game Mary Lane played in after her surgery? The kids were so inspired and uplifted by her courage and determination that it didn't even matter to them when they lost."

"Yeah, I enjoy those kinds of games," Patrick agrees.

"Then why doesn't everybody make more of an effort to have those kinds of games instead of focusing on the scoreboard all the time?" Alecia asks.

What can Alecia and Patrick do to make sports a more inspiring and uplifting experience for everyone in their sports community?

HELP YOUR CHILDREN BE INSPIRED BY THEIR SPORTS EXPERIENCES

You and your children are more likely to be inspired and uplifted by your sports experiences when you feel invested in what you are doing and close to those with whom you are sharing the experiences. The ability to become deeply involved and closely connected can make your family's sports experiences much more enjoyable. Some children naturally throw their whole selves — body and soul —into their sport activities; for others, it requires a greater effort. What can you do to help your children become more personally invested in their sports and in their sports community?

- Help your children learn to enjoy sports for their own sake, not for where sports will get them. Be alert for opportunities (such as driving to and from practice) where you can emphasize the fun in the process, not the rewards of the outcomes. To do so, you need to encourage and guide your children in developing language and images that allow them to experience sports as a journey, rather than a destination. (For example, when you speak of sports, do you focus on things like improvement, courage, determination, and challenge—which emphasize the journey, or is the talk centered around winning, scoring, etc.—which emphasize the destination?)

- Urge your children to help and encourage others. They shouldn't be so focused on winning or on their own performances that they forget to encourage their teammates or to help a fallen opponent off the ground.

- Inspire them to show interest in other people. Young children, especially, love to tell others what is happening in their lives, and that's okay. But teach them to first ask others to share their lives with them by asking questions, such as, "What did you think about how we played today?"

- Show your children how much enjoyment you get from your involvement in a sports event or activity. Let them see you jumping up and down and cheering your favorite team. Point out how much fun certain athletes seem to have when they play.

- Make the effort to get to know other parents and children in your youth sports community so that you can work together to make the community truly vibrant.

EXERCISE

Inspirational stories abound (although you often have to dig past the stories of contract disputes and athletes on trial to find them). As a family assignment, ask each member to look through newspapers or sports magazines to find a story that really touches their spirit. Share these stories with one another at your next family meeting.

Discussion:

Some questions to raise when family members are sharing their inspirational stories include: What touched you most about this story? What can you learn from this story? How does this story change how you look at sports? Does this story teach you anything about getting more joy out of sports and/or life? Does this story make it easier for you to not focus so much attention on winning or the scoreboard? If so, how?

SELF-ASSESSMENT

• What is it that you find inspiring about sports? Are there things that you can do to add to your list of inspiring sports moments?

• Are you really committed to focusing on the inspirational side of sports, versus the outcome-oriented, winning side of sports? Do you communicate this commitment to your children?

• If you feel you are too focused on winning, can you share those feelings with your children? Would you be willing to ask them to work with you to gain a greater appreciation of what sports have to offer?

HOW TO DEVELOP RITUALS OF CELEBRATION

Alecia is looking through some old scrapbooks. "Patrick, remember this?" Alecia asks. "It was the pizza party we had after Darren's Pee Wee team won its first game."

Patrick smiles. "Yeah, I remember. For the rest of the season, they did that little dance after each win."

Alecia continues. "And with Rochelle's first team, it was a team cheer they did when they won. How did that go?"

"You can go East! You can go West! But South Side Strikers are the best!" Alecia and Patrick finish the cheer together. Alecia points out another picture.

"Here's one of the Recognition Banquets the parents used to do. Those were so much fun, watching each of the girls march up to receive her special recognition — why don't we do those anymore?"

"I don't know," Patrick replies. "I think parents and coaches are busier than they used to be, and, to be honest, more focused on winning. And then the kids have gotten more grown-up. They don't seem to want that kind of 'kid' stuff anymore."

"Well, I think we should start doing some of these things again," Alecia asserts.

What benefits do shared rituals bring to the sports setting? What can Alecia and Patrick do to develop meaningful and enjoyable sports rituals for their family?

ESTABLISHING SPORTS RITUALS

Rituals reinforce those ties that connect family members and teammates to one another. They help create a sense of belonging and support. When you, your children, and their teammates create rituals that are meaningful, every time that ritual is re-enacted it renews the spirit and strengthens your connections. How can you create meaningful sports rituals for both your family and your children's teams?

- Decide what sports rituals accurately reflect the values you want to promote (such as a picnic after the game to promote camaraderie, etc.).

- Establish little, daily rituals as well as "big-event" rituals. For example, one soccer mom traditionally sends off each one of her athletic children (and her athletic husband) with the following admonition: "Good luck. Have fun. Play hard."

- Determine ways you can use rituals to draw closer to others in your sports community. One former college quarterback noted that in high school, some of his football teammates walked a little on the "wild side." What his parents would do was videotape each game and invite the team to their house afterwards to watch the tape and eat pizza. That way, the team members found themselves influenced by this family's values, instead of the other way around.

EXERCISE

At a family meeting, discuss rituals that your family has observed in the sports world. Are there any rituals you have observed that you would like to see incorporated into your family's sports life? Remember that some rituals (like wearing silly hats or painting your body in team colors) may look like fun when someone else does them, but don't really fit your family's personality. You may wish to have your family act out the rituals they create so that they can determine if it's really something they want to do. Afterwards, discuss how everyone felt about the ritual. If words like "stupid" or "embarrassing" crop up, you'd probably better look for a new ritual.

Discussion:

As your family talks about different sports rituals each member has observed, ask yourselves what makes a ritual effective?   Which of these rituals promote your family's values? Which ones fit your family's personality?

SELF-ASSESSMENT

• What experiences have you had with sports rituals? Have they primarily been a source of inspiration or embarrassment?

• What experiences have you had with rituals in other areas of your life (such as religious rituals)? Do these experiences offer any ideas or suggestions for incorporating rituals into your sports life?

• How comfortable have you been in leading rituals throughout your life (such as in saying grace at the dinner table or saying the "Pledge of Allegiance" before a school or civic function)? Would you be comfortable in leading your family in a sports ritual? Would another family member be better able to fulfill that role?

HOW TO HELP YOUR CHILDREN DEVELOP RESPECT FOR THE OPPOSITE SEX

"Patrick, I'm concerned about some things I overheard Darren and his friends saying the other day," Alecia says, as she and her husband get ready for bed.

"Oh, yeah? What's that?" asks Patrick.

"Well, a group of them were outside playing basketball while I was in the kitchen with the window open, and they were giving one of the boys a bad time about not 'scoring' with one of the girls at school. I don't think I'm a prude, but some of the things they were saying were really vulgar and demeaning."

Patrick chuckles. "You know how boys are. They like to think they're hot stuff."

"Well, how would you feel if you overheard some boys talking about Rochelle's anatomy and what they would like to do with it? Hmm?"

What is a responsible way for Alecia and Patrick to help Darren and his teammates adopt a respectful attitude toward women?

HELPING YOUR CHILDREN INFLUENCE THEIR PEER GROUP ATTITUDES TOWARD THE OPPOSITE SEX

When people are in a group, they behave differently (and often less admirably) than when they are by themselves. For example, would the young athletes from a prominent community have set out to "score" with as many girls as possible and keep records of their sexual conquests if they were acting individually? Probably not. As a positive sports parent, you must help your children recognize how groups can influence their actions. Even more importantly, you need to help them develop the confidence, not only to refuse to follow the crowd, but also to attempt to influence their peers' attitudes in a positive way. It is a difficult assignment for a young person to assume, but if they do not learn to assert themselves at an early age, it is unlikely they will develop that quality later in life.

Individuals who are most susceptible to being influenced by their peers' attitudes towards the opposite sex are those who fear disapproval and rejection. However, even people who are generally independent and who have high self-esteem have been known to get caught up in a kind of group fervor that leads to acts of sexual exploitation.

Symptoms of an Unhealthy Peer Culture That You and Your Children Should Watch For

- Using stereotypes;
- Suppressing rather than expressing doubts about a group standard of sexual conduct;
- Ridiculing those who challenge the group's expectations of its members;
- Developing group rationalizations for their disrespectful behavior (e.g., "I know a lot of my father's friends who are with a different woman every week").

EXERCISE

With your children, read the case study at the beginning of this chapter. Have them put themselves in Darren's place. Help them develop a strategy for challenging their friends to speak and act more respectfully of the opposite sex. This strategy should include what they might say and when and where would be the best time and place to say it.

Discussion:

Ask your children if they have been in similar situations where they have found themselves uncomfortable with the way their friends have dealt with members of the opposite sex. What would help them have the confidence to challenge the group and encourage others to follow their lead? Express to your children your understanding of how difficult it is for them to go against the group, along with your confidence in their ability to lead by example.

SELF-ASSESSMENT

- What were your peer group's attitudes and behaviors in relation to sexual relationships when you were your children's ages? Did you share the attitudes of your peers? Do you have an understanding of how difficult it will be for your children to challenge peer group standards?

- What attitudes toward sex would you like to see your children have? Are you prepared to share your position with your children if they ask you?

- Where do your children's sexual attitudes and conduct rank among all the issues you are concerned about as a sports parent? Is it an issue you feel is worth fighting about?

- Would you feel comfortable discussing the issue of sexual attitudes and behavior with the parents of your children's teammates in an effort to ensure that all of your children are given appropriate guidance?

HOW TO ADDRESS GENDER-EQUITY ISSUES IN SCHOOL SPORTS

"Rochelle, why are you home so early?" Alecia asks. "I thought you had practice after school today."

"Got canceled," Rochelle replies. "The boys needed the gym."

"Again? Didn't this happen a few weeks ago?"

"Yes!" Rochelle responds, making a face. "Every time the guys have a big game, their coach always asks for extra gym time. If we want to practice, we have to do it after the guys are all done, but our coach doesn't like us to be working out that late."

"That's not fair," Alecia says. "You know, I thought Title IX was supposed to get rid of that kind of stuff, but from my experience, it seems like the girls' sports programs are still getting the short end of the stick."

"Yeah, tell me about it!" Rochelle replies.

How should the Hawkinses generate support for achieving gender equity in the schools?

BECOMING AN ADVOCATE FOR GENDER EQUITY

Despite the fact that Title IX (the federal law that prohibits gender discrimination in school sports programs) has been around for more than 25 years, many high school and college athletics programs still provide more resources to the boys' and men's teams. What are some things you can do to become an advocate for gender equity in your children's schools?

- Learn how to recognize when inequities are taking place. Ask yourself, "Are athletic programs funded in proportion to the percentage of male and female students? Are opportunities for male and female athletes proportional to enrollment? Is there an unmet need for a varsity girls' sport?"

- Actively promote gender-equity policies in the school sports program, especially by offering to serve on advisory groups or by collecting information about programs that may have taken some actions themselves to improve similar situations.

- Speak up if you feel your child's school is in violation of Title IX. Discuss the issue with your child's coach first, then if necessary with athletic administrators, the school principal, and other concerned parents.

- If you fail to get satisfaction from school decision makers, you may want to petition the Board of Education or file a complaint with your state representative. If all else fails, you may need to consider filing a complaint with the federal government or filing a suit against the local school district.

- Remember, the best way to proceed is to help everyone involved work toward a win-win solution. When Title IX compliance becomes a "girls against boys" battle, hard feelings abound and everyone loses. However, in some cases a compromise may not be found. You may need to settle upon a win-lose solution to achieve the objective of gender justice.

EXERCISE

Draft a letter to the athletic director (with a copy to the principal) outlining why your family feels it is important for girls to have equal opportunities to participate in school sports. Try to be as constructive as possible, without placing the blame on anyone. Recognize that the AD and the principal also probably recognize the importance of and desire gender equity and that they may be seeking ways that you are unaware of to work toward achieving that goal. Try to make suggestions that allow school officials to move in the direction of equal opportunity while at the same time minimizing the resistance they are going to face from those involved in boys' sports.

Discussion:

Discuss with your family if and when you would want to send the above letter. Your children, especially, might be concerned about "taking the heat" for any attempts on your part to force changes in the school athletic program. To help your family understand both sides of the issue, discuss the factors that have made it difficult for the school to provide equal opportunities for girls and boys. Try to understand what is going through the minds of school officials as they attempt to address gender-equality issues.

SELF-ASSESSMENT

- When you were growing up, what kinds of sports opportunities were available for young girls?   Did your parents think it was good for women to participate in sports? How has the experience of being raised in that era affected your attitudes toward gender equity in sports?

- How important to you is gender equity in sports at this point in your life? How do you think your attitudes about the women's movement are impacting your children's attitudes toward equal opportunities in sports?

- Are you prepared to take the risk of being viewed as a troublemaker to achieve gender equity in your children's sports programs?

- What skills do you feel are needed to become an effective advocate for gender equity in school sports? Do you have these skills? Are you willing to learn them?

HOW TO HELP YOUR CHILDREN
BRIDGE THE GENERATION GAP

"I can't believe the coach sometimes," Rochelle complains one morning. "She is so out of touch! She keeps reminding us about all the sacrifices she had to make when she was playing sports in the 'good old days.' It's all we can do to keep from laughing. She's so weird."

"Define 'weird,'" Alecia probes.

"You know — like someone from one of those old movies you watch, Mom. She stills wears polyester leisure suits, for heaven's sake. And she calls us 'ladies.' Here she is, ready to retire in a year or two, and the women's movement has entirely passed her by."

"I don't know about that," Alecia replies. "If she's been coaching for all these years, I bet she knows more about life than you give her credit for." Rochelle just rolls her eyes.

What can Alecia do to help Rochelle develop an understanding and appreciation for what her coach and others of her generation have experienced?

TEACHING YOUR CHILDREN TO
CONNECT WITH THEIR ELDERS

In modern America, young people of every generation have experienced a significant gap between themselves, their parents, and their grandparents. The faster social change occurs, the larger the gap. Your children, like most of today's young athletes, probably have few opportunities (and little desire) to develop a real understanding of and appreciation for members of previous generations. Sports, however, are ideal for connecting with older people in a way that can be rewarding for everyone, young and old alike.

Steps Toward Connecting the Generations

- When your children comment that an older person, such as their coach, seems "out of touch," encourage them to imagine what experiences that person might have gone through as a young athlete.

- Take time to put your children in touch with athletes of your own and your parents' eras who are willing to share with them their experiences with sports.

- Invite your children to join you in watching replays of sports classics that appear regularly on cable TV (or rent the videotape series Baseball that charts baseball's history, and watch it with your children). Share your early experiences with sports and compare your experiences and your children's experiences with these classics.

EXERCISE

Find an older member of your family or community who participated in sports as a youth. As a family, interview that person to find out: 1) What the sport was like when he/she played (e.g., what kind of equipment they had, how they trained, who they competed against, what kind of uniform they wore, etc.); 2) How the sport has changed since they played; 3) What they learned from playing sports that helped them in life; 4) How they feel sports have changed for the better or the worse since they played. (Perhaps your children can use this interview for one of their school projects.)

Discussion:

Before you conduct your interview, review the above questions with your children. Can they think of additional questions to ask about sports or the person's life in general? Encourage the person you're interviewing to share with you not only the facts about sports, but additional stories about his or her life when he or she were young.

SELF-ASSESSMENT

• How much time do you spend with older people? Do you make a conscious effort to stay connected with older members of your family?

• What have your experiences taught you about how best to connect with your elders? (For instance, some families enjoy making regular visits to nursing homes in their communities, while others are more comfortable befriending elderly neighbors or taking part in regular family reunions.)

• How effective are you in relating to the older generation? What kinds of skills are required for effective cross-generational communication?

• How good are you at helping your children to see the world of sports from your own and your parents' points of view?

• What role do sports play in connecting you with the older generation? Do you, your children, and your parents share common sports experiences? Are there sports outings you could plan that would bring all three generations together?

HOW TO HELP YOUR CHILDREN RESPOND
TO ISSUES OF HOMOSEXUALITY
IN THE SPORTS WORLD

As Patrick walks into the garage to get his car, he finds Darren and Rochelle there. Darren is spotting Rochelle as she carefully lifts a heavy barbell over her head. "Whoo!" Rochelle gasps, as she lowers the weight.

"Did you see that, Daddy? Seventy-five pounds! Feel my muscles!" She holds out her biceps.

Patrick looks at his daughter's arms. "Be careful you don't overdo it, Honey. You don't want to look like some of the swimmers we see on television."

"Why not?" Rochelle asks. "They're really strong. I think it's cool."

Patrick looks at Darren with a "help me out here" expression on his face.

"I think what Dad's trying to say, Rochelle, is that if you get too buffed the guys are gonna think you're a lesbian. You don't want that, do you?"

"What is it with you guys, anyway?" Rochelle fumes. "Do you think every girl who plays sports is a lesbian? And so what if I were?"

What are the Hawkinses' responsibilities in helping their children use their sports experiences to develop an understanding about homosexuality in sports?

HELPING YOUR CHILDREN DEAL
WITH HOMOSEXUALITY IN SPORTS

Fear of being perceived as homosexual causes many young women to forgo athletics and causes many young men to fear expressing feelings and interests that don't lie within the traditional concept of what is considered masculine. Young athletes may wrestle with how to respond to issues of homosexuality in sports. You can best prepare them for a response by eliminating fear and ignorance while emphasizing the importance of respecting the value of human beings. Some of you reading this have very strong convictions that homosexuality violates your moral standards. Others see the issue as one of tolerance, akin to other types of diversity in our society. Still others either are or have friends or family members who are homosexual. Other views than these undoubtedly exist. It is ludicrous to think that at the time of this writing we can all agree on the way homosexuality itself should be viewed. What we can all agree upon, however, is that human life is very valuable and that treating someone badly based on fear or even loathing of a lifestyle is inappropriate. As a parent, you are responsible for setting examples for your children that take into account your family's beliefs and values. You are also responsible for preparing them to understand that the differences among individuals have nothing to do with the way they should be treated, be it in a job, a classroom, or on an athletic team. How can this be accomplished?

• Identify and discuss the stereotypes that people often have about male and female athletes. Behaviors or tendencies that appear more masculine or feminine are not necessarily linked to homosexual or heterosexual orientations.

• Challenge any misunderstandings that your children might hold toward gay and lesbian athletes or coaches (e.g., gay or lesbian athletes or coaches are no more likely to look upon others in a sexual context than heterosexual athletes or coaches).

• Encourage your sons and daughters to avoid viewing certain activities or feelings as exclusively "male" or "female," but to embrace a wide range of opportunities and experiences. Remind your children that while their sexual identities may be assigned at birth, their gender identities (what kind of men or women they want to be) is something they can fashion to flt their unique needs, interests, and values.

EXERCISE

Softball Olympian Dr. Dot Richardson has observed, "I believe the stereotype of female athletes as lesbians has been one of the greatest hindrances in the development of women in sports." As a family, share the experiences you have had that would either support or contradict this observation by the 1996 Olympic team captain. Discuss how you think this stereotype impacts the women who are characterized as "butch" simply because they are athletes. Are all women athletes painted with that same brush, or is it only those women who possess masculine characteristics? Discuss with your family how they feel about athletes, like tennis champion Martina Navratilova or diving champion Greg Louganis who have publicly "come out" and acknowledged their homosexuality. Consider how negative attitudes toward homosexuals in sports affect the gay athlete, the sport, and your family's own enjoyment of the performances of a gay athletes. Ask, "When these negative attitudes exist, who is the *victim*—the gay athlete, the sport, or the person who is unable to enjoy witnessing the performance of gay athletes?"

Discussion:

Ask your children how they would feel if they thought one of their teammates were gay. Would they want to discuss it with you? What questions would they have?

How would they behave toward that teammate? What do your children believe is the best way for a parent to respond to a gay child?

SELF-ASSESSMENT

• When you were growing up, what kinds of attitudes, if any, did you and your friends have about homosexuality in sports? How much knowledge of homosexuality did you have at that time? What terms did you use to describe someone whom you thought was a homosexual?

• How do you now feel when you are in the presence of a person you know or suspect is gay? Why do you think you feel the way you do?

• How confident are you in your ability to help your children understand homosexuality?

HOW TO HELP YOUR CHILDREN COPE
WITH RACISM IN YOUTH SPORTS

Patrick has promised to pick up Darren and some of his friends after practice. He is a little late in arriving. As Patrick approaches the bleachers where the boys are waiting, he hears Darren and his friends talking about their opponents for the upcoming game.

"Man, this is gonna be a tough game," one of the boys says.

"Yeah, I hate playing those 'gang-bangers,' another one comments. "You never know what kind of stuff they're gonna pull."

"Hey, we'll just sic Ricky on them!" Darren laughs. "He's one of them, so he should know what to do!"

Patrick is upset and disappointed at their words. He and Alecia have always tried to instill in their children a deep respect for others, regardless of race, religion, or economic status.

How can Patrick and Alecia bring about change in Darren's unacceptable behavior?

TEACHING YOUR CHILDREN TO VALUE
DIVERSITY IN SPORTS

Youth sports programs are an ideal tool for fighting racism and promoting activities that bring communities together, not tear them apart. You can use the forum of youth sports to help your children appreciate and value each individual's background and heritage. How do you go about doing so?

- With your children, research the history of racism in sports. Discuss the contributions to sports that have been made by individuals of different races.

- Ask your children to describe incidents they have witnessed in their sports experiences that indicate there is still evidence of racism in their sports programs. Invite them to share with you how they felt about these incidents.

- Ask your children to think of actions that they could take that could strengthen relationships between athletes of different races.

- At your children's sporting events, make a point of sitting next to a family who is a different race than you. If you are not already acquainted, introduce yourself so you can learn things about the family that you can share with your children.

EXERCISE

To draw your children's attention to the issue of race relations in sports and help them focus on positive incidents and actions that they can take, assign your children to look for incidents in their sports programs where majority and minority athletes both feel included. Ask them to observe: Who took the initiative? How did the athletes involved benefit from the incident? What impact did the incident have on everyone's sports experiences? Were there any negative consequences from the encounter? Have your children report on the answers to these questions at your next family meeting.

Discussion:

After completing the above exercise, what conclusions have your children drawn about how they can contribute to good race relations in their sports programs? Communicate to your children your expectations that they assume leadership in fighting against misunderstandings between people of different races, whether it be in their sports programs or other areas of their lives.

SELF-ASSESSMENT

- When you were your children's ages, what were the prevailing beliefs about athletes of a different color, nationality, or culture? How did these beliefs affect you?

- When you were a child, how did your group of friends feel about athletes who were different? What kind of peer pressure, if any, did you experience to conform to their views? What kind of peer pressures do your children experience in this day and age?

- What are the roots of your beliefs about other races and cultures? How accurately do you feel these beliefs portray athletes of other races and cultures? Is there someone you can discuss your beliefs with to determine whether you are basing your conclusions on fact or upon stereotypes that were firmly established in your youth?

- What experiences have you had that would allow you to develop rewarding relationships with parents and athletes of different races and cultures?

HOW TO DEVELOP A WORKING RELATIONSHIP WITH THE COACH

Patrick is speaking on the telephone. "Yes," he says, "I talked it over with my family, and I would be happy to be a chaperone for Darren's team this year. I think it will be a lot of fun."

After Patrick hangs up the phone, Alecia smiles and says, "Can you believe with all our years in youth sports, this is the first time one of us has been a chaperone? Are you nervous?"

Patrick shrugs. "I wouldn't be if it was Coach Santera I was working with. We've know him for years. But I don't know what this new coach expects from a chaperone."

"Did he say anything about your responsibilities?" Alecia asks.

"He seemed a little touchy when I asked," Patrick responds. "'Just drive the car' is what he said."

How can Patrick be helpful without "stepping on the coach's toes"?

BUILDING RAPPORT WITH THE COACH

As a positive sports parent, your goal is to make sports an uplifting and enriching experience for your family. To do so, you need to establish a partnership with those men and women who coach your children. However, many coaches today have been so scarred by their experiences with over-zealous parents that they are wary of any parental involvement. What can you do to build positive, productive relationships with your children's coaches?

- Show genuine interest in your children's coaches. Take the time to learn their views on sports and coaching, issues they may have (either with athletes or parents), what they expect from you as a chaperone, problems they have had in the past, etc. (Avoid questions that might put them on the defensive.)
- Meet with the coach at a time and place that is comfortable for both of you. In other words, don't try to corner the coach after practice or a game, when he or she is preoccupied.
- Present yourself as a "team player" who is there to make the coach's job easier.
- When talking to the coach about your child or any other child, always speak positively.
- Remember that building a successful parent/coach relationship is a season-long process. Don't expect to become close after the first meeting.

EXERCISE

(This exercise does not need to involve your children.) With the coach's approval, get together with other team parents and brainstorm how you can be more constructive contributors to the team. Prior to the meeting, discuss the agenda with the coach. Afterwards, report the results of the meeting to the coach. Offer to arrange a meeting between the coach and the team parents to review the suggestions that were made.

Discussion:

If the coach is uncomfortable with the idea of parents meeting alone, encourage him or her to attend the meeting with you. Ask the coach which one of you should conduct the meeting. Good things can happen either with or without the coach. In either case, the question that needs to be raised is, "What can we parents do to get behind the program so that everyone—our kids, the coach, and the team families—gets the most out of this experience?"

SELF-ASSESSMENT

• What experiences have you had in working with coaches in youth sports programs? How might these experiences impact your effectiveness in working with your children's current coaches?

• Do you have confidence in your children's coaches? Why or why not? In what ways do you feel that you can add to the effectiveness of your children's coaches? How much support are you prepared to offer?

• How good are you at establishing rapport with people you don't know? What skills do you need to work on to do better at getting to know people? (For example, do you need to work on overcoming shyness? Do you need to learn how to ask questions that draw people out of themselves? Do you need to be a better listener?)

HOW TO SUPPORT POSITIVE COACHING BEHAVIOR

Last year, Patrick had been dismayed by the actions of one of Darren's coaches, a volatile man who could never seem to get through a contest without getting into a screaming match with an official, an opponent, or one of his own players. As Patrick and Alecia settle into their seats for the opening game of the new season and Patrick spots the coach out on the floor, he sighs. "Here we go again, Alecia. Did you bring my ear plugs?"

However, throughout the close and exciting game, Patrick is surprised to see that the coach is making a visible effort to control his temper.

"Can you believe it?" Patrick asks, as the game ends. "He never yelled. Not once."

Alecia laughs. "Well, why don't you go tell him how much you appreciated his behavior?"

Patrick shakes his head. "Nah, I couldn't do that. What if he took it wrong?"

What can Patrick and Alecia do to support and encourage their children's coaches to act in ways that are in line with the principles of positive sports parenting?

LEARNING THE ART OF POSITIVE SUPPORT

Any child behavioral specialist will tell you that one of the best ways to encourage positive behavior in children is to catch them doing something good and immediately reward them. Adults are no different. Too often, parents only make comments to coaches when something negative happens. Parents who want their children's coaches to coach in a positive, supportive way need to go out of their way to give recognition to behavior that fits this pattern. You can do so by:

- Developing criteria for determining what constitutes positive coaching behavior. (Since you might not be an impartial judge, get feedback from others on these criteria.)
- Becoming a patient observer. Don't make snap judgments regarding a coach based on one or two minor incidents.
- Remembering that which gets praised gets repeated. Don't hesitate to praise the coach's positive behavior directly to the coach, to other parents and fans, to the athletes, and to the coach's superiors.
- Encouraging other parents to support positive coaching behavior. For example, "You know, I'm really impressed with the way the coach handled your child's anxiety after that hard hit. When you talk to the coach, you can add my compliments to yours."

EXERCISE

Take a notebook with you to your child's next competition. Write down all the things the coach does that are examples of positive coaching behavior. Pick one or two of these items to compliment the coach on after the competition.

Discussion:

In providing support for your coach's positive behavior, you need to be careful how you communicate the message. Otherwise, your initiative might be interpreted as a challenge to the coach's usual way of doing business. (For example, saying something like, "I was really impressed with the enthusiasm you showed for the reserves when they came off the field tonight," will probably be received a lot better than, "Wow, you finally let some of the reserve players get in the game. Good job!") If you're in doubt about how a comment or action might be received, discuss it with your partner or another team parent. Ask them how it would make them feel if they were the coach.

SELF-ASSESSMENT

- How would you characterize the coaching you received when you were involved in sports? Were your coaches generally positive or negative? How did you respond to the different coaching styles?

- When you have tried to teach a skill (sports or otherwise) to children, what approach have you found to be most effective — one who accentuates the positive or one who points out errors and shortcomings? Do you feel that your children respond better to threats or rewards?

- How are your experiences in observing how your own children respond to different coaching styles affecting your expectations for their current coaches? Do you genuinely believe that positive coaching behavior will work best for your children and their team?

- How would you describe your relationship with your children's coaches? Have you been able to establish open, mutually supportive relationships? Do you feel comfortable in encouraging their positive coaching behavior?

HOW TO HELP INTEGRATE THE
ISOLATED ATHLETE INTO THE LIFE OF THE TEAM

"Hey, Mom, is it okay if I have a sleep over next Saturday night for the team?" Rochelle asks her mother after school one day.

"We've got to go over to Aunt Joan's house Saturday night — it's her birthday. How about Friday night instead? That way you girls could all just come over here straight from practice."

Rochelle frowns. "Yeah, but then Marion will come, too."

Alecia looks puzzled. "Well, you did say you were inviting the team, didn't you?"

"Yes, but I really didn't want her to come, Mom. She's so weird."

Alecia sits down at the table. "You know, Rochelle, I notice that no one talks to Marion very much at the games or the practices. Why is that?"

"Like I said, Mom — she's weird. She tries to make jokes and they're not funny, or she'll come out with the most off-the-wall remarks. No one knows what to say to her."

What steps should Alecia take when she sees players socially isolating a teammate?

HELPING EVERYONE FEEL INCLUDED

Belonging to a group is part of the way children form values and establish their identities. Unfortunately, this need to belong can often lead to hurt feelings and loss of self-esteem on the part of those who are excluded from the group. As a positive sports parent, there are steps you can take to ensure that all team members feel as if they are part of the same group and to help your own children reach out to those who are being isolated. These steps might include:

- Making a special effort to get to know the athlete who is not part of the group;

- Looking for special talents or abilities the child might have that you can bring to the attention of the other children;

- Looking for ways you can include the isolated athlete in some of your family activities;

- Discussing the problem with the coach and figuring out ways the coach can build the isolated athlete's self-esteem and help him or her interact with other team members;

- Building your own children's self-esteem (children with high self-esteem are less likely to exclude others);

- Helping your children to get to know a variety of children by suggesting that they sit by different people at every practice;

- Supporting your children as positive role models (for example, if your children are well liked, explain that they can use their stature in the group to build greater team unity).

- Talking to your children about the value and potential benefits of reaching out to someone who is not part of the group.

EXERCISE

In collaboration with the coach, call a team meeting with the expressed purpose of trying to build team unity. Ask the athletes to recall a time when they were left out. How did they feel? In contrast, how do they feel when someone includes them or makes them feel welcome? Ask them to list three things they could do to build team unity so that all members of the team feel closely connected to one another.

Discussion:

Urge the athletes to be specific and detailed about the incidents they are reporting. Remind them to talk only about things that happened to them, not to other people. Take care that the athletes not identify anyone on the present team as an outsider. Instead, discuss with the athletes the benefits of having a cohesive team where everyone feels like they are part of a united effort.

SELF-ASSESSMENT

• How effective are you at building unity in the groups to which you belong? What leadership techniques have you found most effective in getting everyone moving in the same direction? Since techniques that work with adults can be ineffective with young people, what techniques do you think might work in building unity on your child's team?

• Have you ever been part of a group that shunned another person? What were the reasons for doing so? How did it make you feel? If you could go back and do things differently, what would you change?

• How can you use your experiences in either being part of the group or apart from the group to help build unity on your children's teams?

46

HOW TO HELP TEAM MEMBERS COMMUNICATE WITH THEIR COACH

Patrick, who has been designated as the team parent for an upcoming trip, is driving a few of Darren's teammates home from practice when he overhears the following conversation.

"Can you believe the coach, demoting Jackson to the second team?" Jimmy exclaims.

"It doesn't make any sense. All that he did was to be late for a couple of practices," Sean angrily responds. "And he had a good reason for being late, too!"

"Doesn't matter now. Without Jackson, we don't stand a chance against Newhall next week," Jimmy comments.

"The coach is just trying to be hard nosed," Sean says. "What do you think he would do if we sent Latrell to talk to him? Latrell's team captain — maybe he could get Coach to change his mind."

Darren snorts. "It's more likely that Coach would throw Latrell out of his office."

"Man, we've got to do something," Jimmy moans. "That Newhall game will be tough enough, even if we do have Jackson in the starting lineup. What do you think, Mr. Hawkins? Do you think the coach would pay any attention to Latrell if he tried to talk to him?"

How should Patrick respond? Should he offer to coach the boys on how to present their case? Should he speak to the coach on the team's behalf? What are the risks he runs with each of these options?

FACILITATING COMMUNICATION BETWEEN ATHLETES AND COACHES

When athletes are having problems with a coach, it doesn't necessarily mean that the coach is a bad person or even a bad coach. Parent leaders are often in a position to make communication between athletes and coaches an easier and more successful process. To encourage athletes to communicate openly with the coach, you can:

- Ask the athletes how they see themselves reacting when presented with a new idea or a different viewpoint (e.g., are they open-minded, closed-minded, defensive?). Then ask them how they would see the coach reacting under the same circumstances.

- Help them determine what they want from the coach. Do they want the coach to acknowledge their concerns? Do they want the coach to explain some of his or her actions? Do they want specific changes to occur?

- Help the athletes develop a game plan. Will they make an appointment with the coach? Will they write a letter? Will they notify the coach of their concerns prior to meeting with him or her? How many athletes will attend the meeting?

- Role play with the athletes how the meeting will go. Explore several possibilities.

EXERCISE

With the consent of the coach, hold a meeting with the team to discuss your role as a team parent in promoting effective communication between the athletes and the coach. Ask the athletes to identify, on the basis of their experiences with other coaches, breakdowns in communication they have experienced. Using these examples, ask the group to determine whether it was a communication problem (for example, the coach didn't give clear instructions) or a problem that reflected significant differences in opinion (the coach felt that any kind of questions from the athletes were insubordination, while the athletes felt they should be able to express reasonable objections). Next, ask the athletes to discuss what steps could have been taken to effectively deal with those problems that arose as a result of communication breakdowns. Ask them to think of some specific strategies that could be put into place that will reduce the likelihood of having communication problems with their current coach.

Discussion:

Explain to the team that most misunderstandings result from faulty communication. In addition, help them understand that communication is a two-way street; both they and their coach have to do their part. Ask them if they feel comfortable in presenting their list of effective communication strategies to their coach. Encourage the coach to meet with the team or team leaders to put into place procedures designed to open up the channels of communication.

SELF-ASSESSMENT

• How comfortable are you in serving as an ambassador to encourage communication between the athletes and the coach? Are you able to deal with the possibility that the coach may blame you for any bad news you communicate?

• How effective do you think you will be in coaching team leaders how to be advocates for their team's interests? How good are your listening skills? How good are your teaching skills? How good are your negotiating skills?

• Are you able to stay neutral in your role, without seeming to side with one party or another?

HOW TO HELP TEAM MEMBERS
RESPECT PROPERTY RIGHTS

After a regional competition, Patrick is driving Darren and several of his team-mates home. At one point, Patrick hears some whispering and giggling coming from the back of the van. "Hey Mitch, where did you put it?" one of the boys asks in a hushed voice.

"It's here in my laundry bag," Mitch replies. "I'll show you when we get home."

As Patrick wonders what "it" is, he hears another boy say, "Cool! We've never been able to swipe a Nike banner before!"

"Shh!" Darren says, nodding his head in Patrick's direction.

What action should Patrick take in this instance? How can these kinds of incidents be averted?

PREVENTING VANDALISM

Young athletes are profoundly impacted by the standards that are estab-lished by their groups. If it is commonplace among the athletes on the team to steal banners at competitions or sneak hotel towels into their bags on a road trip, it is likely that you as a parent leader will be faced with the challenge of having to police such actions. On the other hand, children who are members of a group that has made a conscious commitment not to engage in destructive and illegal activities seldom vandalize. Positive sports parents reject such ra-tionalizations as "kids will be kids" (or that one little towel won't be missed) and take actions to reduce the chances of athletes engaging in theft or vandalism.

Some things you can do include:

- Holding a team meeting with coaches and athletes at the beginning of the season for the purpose of establishing team rules. Insist that the team examine such issues (like vandalism, or trash talk) that are too often accepted as standard behavior in the sports world. Encourage them to set high standards.

- Having the team address such questions as 1) What rules should we have? 2) Who should police athlete behavior? 3) If an athlete steals or vandalizes something, what should the consequences be? 4) What should the consequences be for someone who knows of the violation but doesn't report it? 5) Who is responsible for administering the punishment?

- Having team parents review the rules and agree to encourage their children to adhere to these standards.

- Helping the team find other outlets for their energy, such as taking part in a community service project. This will help them feel connected to their community in a positive way and less likely to feel the need to challenge authority.

EXERCISE

As a team project, ask each athlete to interview one local official, school administrator, hotel manager, police officer, building superintendent, restaurant manager, parks and recreation administrator, janitor, or someone else who deals with vandalism and theft on a frequent basis. Have the athletes compare their answers in a follow-up meeting. Complete this exercise prior to establishing team rules of conduct.

Discussion:

At the follow-up meeting, discuss the costs of theft and vandalism, the magnitude of the problem, and the effect it has on its victims. Did learning about how vandalism and theft affect real individuals (versus impersonal organizations) change how the team members view this problem?

SELF-ASSESSMENT

• When you were a young athlete, did you or your friends engage in acts of vandalism? What was your attitude toward vandalism when you were young? What is your attitude now? If your attitude has changed over the years, what has caused the change?

• How comfortable are you in asking that athletes adhere to a strict code of conduct? Will it bother you if your opinions make you unpopular with some of the athletes?

• How skilled would you be in working with a group of young athletes to establish rules of conduct? Is there anyone who could give you helpful advice on how to organize and conduct this kind of meeting?

HOW TO HELP PARENTS APPRECIATE THE BENEFITS OF POSITIVE SPORTS PARENTING

"Well, Mrs. Hawkins," Rochelle's coach is saying, "thank you for agreeing to serve as chaperone for the team. I think you'll be a good role model for some of our other parents."

"Oh, really?" Alecia responds, surprised.

"Yes, we have a few who can be very vocal sometimes," the coach comments.

At the next game, Alecia sees what the coach means. After a poor call, one of the parents gets so upset he almost runs onto the court to assault the official. Even after the parent is restrained, he continues to yell at the official for several minutes.

What can Alecia do to help other parents understand and apply positive sports parenting principles in their own lives?

INFLUENCING OTHER SPORTS PARENTS

One sports psychologist noted that his most popular lecture to coaches is "Parents from Hell." Many coaches and parents have observed that it is getting harder and harder to convince parents to act appropriately when their children are on the field. As a positive sports parent, you can help influence other parents to rein in their competitive juices. How?

- Help other parents see what's in it for them (in other words, help them see how positive sports parenting can make their family's sports experience more enjoyable).

- Be an understanding fellow team parent. When other parents feel that you sincerely care about them, they will be more inclined to follow your example.

- Address conduct issues before the season begins. Get parents to agree on what kind of action should be taken when a parent gets out of hand.

- Build a sense of camaraderie in the parent community so that everyone can be guided by a common set of agreed-upon sports values.

- Model positive parenting behavior. Let other parents see you greet the opposing coach, wish his or her team good luck, and compliment good plays by the opposing players. Emphasize effort over results.

- Allow frustrated parents to vent their feelings to you. Say, "I understand," and then be quiet — don't argue.

- Encourage parents to sleep on any decisions they might be considering, such as withdrawing their children from the program because of lack playing time. This strategy reduces the chance that they will embarrass themselves or be a disruptive force in the parent community.

- If you must speak to parents about their behavior, talk to them privately. Embarrassing them or putting them on the defensive will not accomplish your goal.

EXERCISE

Before the start of the sports season, conduct a mandatory parent meeting to establish a parents' code of conduct. Prior to the meeting talk to the coach to find out what issues he or she would like to have discussed at the meeting. Be sure these items are included on your agenda at the meeting:

- Raise issues that need to be addressed. These may include such things as parental responsibility for getting athletes to practice on time; procedures for filing complaints with the coach; and bleacher conduct.

• Invite parents to add additional issues to the list.

• Divide parents into small groups. Assign each group one or two issues and ask them to come up with appropriate guidelines.

• Discuss the suggested guidelines with the entire group. Make changes as needed. Hold a vote to adopt the code. (If the coach is not able to participate in the meeting, he or she should be provided with a draft of the code prior to its adoption.)

Discussion:

Ask the parents for their suggestions on how you can all encourage each other in your efforts to maintain positive sports parenting behavior. For example, the group may decide to come up with a code word or phrase that can be used when a parent's behavior is veering toward the negative. The important thing is to get parents working together to create a positive sports climate.

SELF-ASSESSMENT

• What are some challenges you might face in encouraging parents to adopt a parental code of conduct? How might you respond to these challenges?

• Do you feel that you are a good example of a positive sports parent?

• What skills do you have that can make you an effective positive sports parent leader? What skills do you need to improve?

49

HOW TO BE SENSITIVE TO FAMILIES WITH SPECIAL NEEDS

Alecia and Sharon, another team mom, are meeting to discuss the annual fundraiser for Darren's team. It is the second year in a row that they have been in charge of it.

"I guess we did such a great job last year, they figured why rock the boat?" Alecia smiles.

"No one else has the time or energy for it," Sharon complains. "Lexi and Chavonne have their hands full trying to take care of their families by themselves, and the other moms all have full-time jobs, too, so even if they aren't single parents they're still practically as busy as one."

"But we do have a good group of parents, and they want to help," Alecia says. "Lexi was telling me that she wishes she felt more a part of the group, but it's so hard for her right now. We just need to figure out a way to include everyone, without adding to their stress — or ours!"

How can Alecia help her children's sports programs adapt to a society where the majority of children are from families with single parents and working mothers?

HELPING ALL TEAM PARENTS FEEL INCLUDED

Besides the normal stresses that any parent has to deal with, single parents and working mothers often feel the added stress of guilt that they're not doing enough for their children, especially when it comes to participating in their children's youth sports programs. As a parent leader who wants to help single parents and working mothers feel more included in their children's sports programs, it is important to:

- Encourage the coach to underscore the importance of parental participation in the program.
- Help parents become acquainted with one another so they can develop ways to share team responsibilities.
- Reach out to all parents. Informal gatherings with children present are almost always effective in building bonds among parents.
- Identify common interests and/or parenting issues to help you choose topics for parent meetings. Give special attention to the challenges of managing time in a way that allows all team parents opportunities to enjoy participating in their children's sports programs.
- Invite all parents to identify the boundaries of their availability, and then organize parent support tasks accordingly.

EXERCISE

- Plan a potluck or some other kind of gathering where team families can get to know one another better. To ensure a successful gathering, your action plan should include:
- Written invitations with a telephone follow-up to ensure maximum attendance;
- A reminder sent home by the coach on meeting day (prepared by a parent leader);
- Name tags;
- A written agenda (if business is to be conducted);
- Clear time limits (e.g., 7-9 p.m.) that you stick to!

Discussion:

At your get-togethers, try playing a "getting acquainted" game, such as where the parents have to find someone in the group who: 1) has the same number of children; 2) shares the same number of letters in their last name; or 3) shares the same high school graduation year, city, or school (you can think of more ideas along these lines). Afterwards, ask parents to share one thing that they learned about someone else.

SELF–ASSESSMENT

• What attitudes and beliefs do you have regarding single parents and/or working mothers? How do these views affect your relationships with other team parents?

• How good are you at making everyone feel a part of your community of parents? Why do you think you are good or not so good? Would you be willing to survey parents (such as distributing an anonymous question-naire for them to complete) to get feedback on your effectiveness as a parent leader?

50

HOW TO ENCOURAGE PARENTAL INVOLVEMENT IN YOUTH SPORTS PROGRAMS

Some of the parents of Rochelle's teammates seem to take little interest in their daughters' sports activities. This bothers Patrick and Alecia, who, as parent leaders, would like to see all of the parents supporting the team.

"I don't understand," Patrick says one day. "These parents seem caring, but when it comes to getting involved with the program, they never show up. I can understand being busy and not able to participate in every activity, but when you start missing games on a regular basis — I mean, how can they do that to their kids?"

"I don't like to think it is a sexist thing," Alecia says, "but I bet if it were their sons' program they'd be there for them."

"I don't know," Patrick replies. "There are parents who don't show up for Darren's games, too. A lot of them are the same ones who never lift a finger to help with fund raising or anything else, no matter how much we work to accommodate their schedules and stuff. So I don't think it's a lack of time; I think it's a lack of interest."

"That's a tough one," Alecia says. "How do we get them interested?"

What can Patrick and Alecia do to motivate other parents to become more involved in their children's sports programs?

BUILDING A SENSE OF COMMUNITY AMONG PARENTS

When parents aren't very involved in their children's sports program, one factor could be their lack of connection to the program. Perhaps they don't know the other parents or kids very well, or they never had much interest in sports as children, and that affects how they view their child's sports involvement. Some parents have never liked sports or feel uncomfortable because they don't know much about a sport. The challenge for parent leaders is to create an attractive and inviting sports community that draws these other parents to it. The strategy you choose should include ideas that (1) remove roadblocks that prevent parents from getting involved; (2) show parents the vital role they play in the program; and (3) provide parents with opportunities to take ownership in the program. You can begin by following these steps:

- Allocate enough time to build a strong team community. You can't create the ideal sports community overnight.

- Identify the things that prevent parents from becoming more involved in the sports community (e.g., work, family priorities, church commitments, dislike of sports, etc.), then develop strategies for minimizing their impact on participation.

- Identify common goals and how the team community can help families meet these goals. For example, everyone wants to strengthen their relationships with their children; sports communities offer parents the chance to share concerns and advice.

EXERCISE

In a formal or informal parent meeting, ask parents to share experiences they've had with being part of strong, attractive communities (these don't have to be sports communities — they can be neighborhoods, churches, or civic groups, etc.). Ask them to identify what features of these communities made it attractive to them and to others. Brainstorm ways you can incorporate these features into your youth sports program. Select a small group of parents to come up with a plan for carrying out these suggestions. (Since the formation of a vital parent community is a key part of a successful youth program, you may want to consider asking the coach to make this meeting an enrollment requirement. Consider holding one mandatory meeting prior to the start of the season, at which such issues as parental involvement and a parental code of conduct can be discussed.)

Discussion:

Ask parents how they would describe an ideal sports community. Ask them how they think their children would describe an ideal sports community. How does your team community measure up to the ideal for parents and children? How much desire is there on the part of parents to bring your team community closer to the ideal?

SELF-ASSESSMENT

• How well do you know the other parents in your group? Do you feel that there is much common ground between you and the other parents? How many things can you think of that you all share, besides wanting the best sports experiences for your children?

• How skilled are you at incorporating "difficult" parents into the parent community without driving the other parents away? Do you know enough about all the parents that you can bring up interests that they share, thus encouraging them to get to know one another?

• What skills do you feel are needed to build a supportive sports parent community? If you don't have these skills, can you think of other parents in the group who do? Would you be willing to ask for their help?

51

HOW TO HELP PARENTS BECOME STUDENTS OF THEIR CHILDREN'S SPORTS

Some of the parents who attend Rochelle's games obviously don't know much about the sport. Not only is this evidence that they have invested little effort in their daughter's sport, but it is also embarrassing to the girls when their parents make uninformed comments.

At one game, after some particularly clueless and loud remarks by one of the dads, Patrick whispers to Alecia: "This guy better shut up before he makes a complete idiot of himself. Look at his daughter out there — she looks like she wants to cry!"

"He means well," Alecia says. "But face it, honey. He obviously never competed in this sport when he was growing up."

"Well, neither did I," Patrick replies, "but I made the effort to learn about it."

"And you enjoy the competition a lot more as a result, don't you?"

"Absolutely. It brought Rochelle and me closer together, too. So what can we do to help some of these other parents make the same discovery?"

As parent leaders, what can Alecia and Patrick do to encourage other parents to become more sports-savvy?

ENCOURAGING SPORTS AWARENESS IN PARENTS

Most parents go to great lengths to support their children's efforts in sports. They shell out money for fees and uniforms, they spend countless hours in the car driving to and from practices, and they yell themselves hoarse during games.

However, not all parents are knowledgeable about the wide variety of sports in which their children participate. This can make it difficult for parents to understand what goals the coaches and athletes are trying to achieve and how they are trying to achieve them. What can parent leaders do to help other parents "get on the same page" as their athletic children?

- Ask the coach to meet with parents early in the season to explain what he or she hopes to accomplish during the season, as well as what individual and team goals have been set.
- Ask the coach if he or she could provide a seminar for parents to familiarize them with the basics of the game.
- Ask a knowledgeable parent to put together a simple one- or two-page handout explaining the basic rules and procedures of the game.
- Invite a knowledgeable parent to give a brief (5 or 10 minutes) "lesson in the stands" to parents before each game, focusing on one aspect of the game.
- Invite your children to plan and conduct a clinic for the team parents.

EXERCISE

Conduct an informal parent survey to determine how many parents would like to know more about their children's sport, and how they feel they could best learn what they need to know (e.g., by means of seminars, handouts at the games, mini-lessons, etc.). Working with the coach and one or two knowledgeable parents, plan what you will do to expand the sports knowledge of your parent community.

Discussion:

As you are planning, you need to ask each other: "How can we best make the learning experience fun and non-threatening?" What are the experience levels in our group? What is the best way to reach each group? (For example, you may need to divide parents into three groups: experienced, novice, and those with some background in the sport.)

SELF-ASSESSMENT

• How knowledgeable are you about your children's sports? Do you demonstrate an eagerness to learn more?

• If you were to choose a sport for your children to participate in, would it be the same sport(s) they have chosen? Why or why not? How much enthusiasm do you have for the sports your children play? If you are less than enthusiastic about a sport, can you be enthusiastic about the opportunities that sport is offering your children? Is your enthusiasm contagious?

52

HOW TO HELP FAMILIES UNDERSTAND THE VALUE OF TEAM LOYALTY

Darren calls Patrick at work. "Dad, guess what? I got a call from Coach Brown of the Titans. He wants me to consider joining his team! Isn't that great?"

"But, Darren, you've already been practicing with your team for a month. You can't switch now."

"Dad, this is the chance of a lifetime! The Titans won the league championship last year, and all of their seniors got scholarships to top schools. Being on their team would guarantee me a scholarship."

"Yes, but you're the team captain, Darren. If you left, what effect would that have on your team and on your coach? They're really counting on you this year."

"But I have to think of myself, too," Darren responds. "That's what the pros do."

"Let's talk about it more when I get home," Patrick says.

As a parent leader, how should Patrick handle Darren's dilemma? How can he prepare other parents for these kinds of situations?

ETHICS AND FAMILY DECISIONS

In the normal course of a sports career, families are faced with decisions that require them to call upon their moral resources. For example, a moral dilemma arises whenever the benefits to the family have to be weighed against the costs of their actions to others. The act of changing teams is one such dilemma. As a parent leader, you need to work with the other parents to help them consider the consequences of their children's decisions to leave their teams. As they struggle with the issue of team loyalty, you can invite them to:

• Identify the people who could be impacted by a child's decision to leave the team and make an effort to view the decision through their eyes.

• If possible, consult with those who could be affected by a decision to switch teams; doing so will help others feel like they have been part of the decision-making process.

• Identify the ethical principles that need to be considered in "team jumping" cases. Does "do unto others what you would have them do unto you" work in cases of this kind?

• Consider the question of who should ultimately make decisions of this type: athletes, parents, or parents and athletes jointly.

• Determine what role coaches should play in the decision.

EXERCISE

As a topic for discussion with team parents, select a high-profile team-jumping case from personal knowledge or newspaper accounts and prepare a series of questions to discuss. Questions might include: Do you think the athlete made the right decision? Why or why not? How might the athlete's leaving affect the former team's chemistry? The new team's? What advice would you have given to the parents of the athlete when the family was making the decision? Does loyalty really have a place in sports anymore? Why or why not?

Discussion:

To conclude the above discussion, ask parents if they feel there are times when joining a new team is justified. Make a list of when the decision to leave a team is justified and is not justified.

SELF-ASSESSMENT

• During your sports career, were you ever faced with the issue of team loyalty? How did you resolve it? How do your personal experiences with loyalty issues, both in and out of sports, impact your position on team loyalty?

• How can you present your position on loyalty to the other parents in a way that encourages them to openly express their views on the subject?

• Do you feel that professional and college athletes have become increasingly "me" oriented vs. "team" oriented? How comfortable are you with the status of sports today as they relate to loyalty? As a parent leader, what can you do to advance your position on loyalty in sports?

Establish Your Own Positive Sports Parenting Program!

You are committed to taking sports to a higher level, but how can your school or club join you in creating a youth sports climate that brings the best out of everyone—athletes, coaches, and parents? The Positive Sports Parenting Program provides hands-on advice for guiding children to experiencing sports in ways that not only build their bodies, but enrich their lives, too!

Starting a Positive Sports Parenting Program in your community is easy!

Step 1: Tell your local youth sports leader (perhaps a school administrator or club director) about Positive Sports Parenting and ask that leader to contact the Positive Sports Parenting national office at (281) 565-2234.

Step 2: We will help your local youth sports leader identify two to four parents who will receive specialized training from the Positive Sports Parenting staff. This training prepares parents to become Positive Sports Parenting Program Leaders.

Step 3: The Positive Sports Parenting Program Leaders will recruit and train additional parents to become High-Five Team Facilitators.

Step 4: High-Five Team Facilitators will use this book, <u>From the Bleachers with Love,</u> along with a companion workbook, to hold sports parenting workshops with small groups of parents within the school, club, or team.

Take the first step toward more Positive Sports Parenting for your children!

CONTACT:
Positive Sports Parenting • P.O. Box 1429 • Sugar Land, TX 77478
Phone (281) 565-2234 •Fax (281) 565-2224

From The Bleachers With Love

Advice to Parents with Kids in Sports

David Canning Epperson, Ph.D. and George A. Selleck, Ph.D.

Principles of Positive Sports Parenting

Sports courts, fields, and arenas can be so much more than places for keeping kids off the streets. Well-orchestrated school and youth sports programs have the potential of renewing the spirits of participants, teaching life's lessons, and strengthening family and community ties.

This book helps parents take advantage of sports' full range of possibilities for teaching life's lessons and strengthening the family and community. It provides the basis for an ongoing dialogue about how families can get the most out of their sports experiences. In short, it equips parents to add value to their family's investment in sports.

Praise for Beyond the Bleachers

"Since I believe that parenting is the most important profession in the world, I am excited to see that someone has finally written the definitive 'playbook' for sports parents!"

–John Wooden, Legendary Head Basketball Coach, UCLA

"Even more satisfying than watching your child win Wimbledon is watching her grow into a gracious, caring individual. Every parent should be so lucky. By following the advice in Beyond the Bleachers, parents will know that they have done everything possible to make sports a positive influence in their child's life."

–Ann Davenport, Mother of Lindsey Davenport
Wimbledon Champion